WHY THE
DALAI LAMA
IS A
SOCIALIST

WHY THE DALAI LAMA IS A SOCIALIST

BUDDHISM AND THE COMPASSIONATE SOCIETY

Terry Gibbs

ZED

Zed Books

LONDON

Why the Dalai Lama is a Socialist: Buddhism and the Compassionate Society
was first published in 2017 by Zed Books Ltd,
The Foundry, 17 Oval Way, London SE11 5RR, UK.

www.zedbooks.net

Copyright © Terry Gibbs 2017

The right of Terry Gibbs to be identified as the author of this work
has been asserted by her in accordance with the Copyright,
Designs and Patents Act, 1988.

Typeset in Haarlammer by seagulls.net
Index by Ed Emery
Cover design by Jonathan Pelham
Cover photo © Danny Martindale/Getty Images

A catalogue record for this book is available from the British Library.

ISBN 978-1-78360-645-0 hb
ISBN 978-1-78360-644-3 pb
ISBN 978-1-78360-646-7 pdf
ISBN 978-1-78360-647-4 epub
ISBN 978-1-78360-648-1 mobi

CONTENTS

ACKNOWLEDGEMENTS

On the cover of this book we see the Dalai Lama holding his hands together in *anjali*, an ancient Indian gesture of offering and of honouring the sacredness of each human being and the earth itself. This simple hand gesture is a symbolic way of recognizing on the spot our profound interdependence as human beings. I write this book in honour of His Holiness the 14th Dalai Lama, whose life and work remind us all to wake up, celebrate our lives and, most of all, to care deeply for one another and for this beautiful planet we call home. In addition to the Dalai Lama, there are many people that have influenced my worldview and who have supported my work over the years, far too many to mention here. But I would like in particular to thank my mother Mair who taught me to live life to the fullest and to always appreciate the present moment and my father Richard who influenced me to take risks and to explore the world – diolch yn fawr iawn! My sisters Maryanne, Ted, Kath, Ern and Jac and my brother Rick have all been an inspiration to me each in their own ways and I have appreciated their openness to my radical ideas and activities and their ongoing support of my various projects. I would also like to thank my step-daughter Johan and grandkids Kathleen and Dylan for grounding our family's heart in Latin America. I owe special thanks to my long-time friend Kirby Evans who introduced me to Karl Marx and was a critical influence in the development of my political ideas and our mutual friend Kevin Coleman who taught me to be militant when necessary in the service of justice. I would also like to thank Lee-Anne Broadhead, Amber Buchanan, JoAnn Citrigno, Carolyn Claire, Tracey Harris, Julie Hearn, Sean Howard, Evelyn Jones, Steve Law, Rebecca MacDonald, Suzanne MacNeil, Kirk Morrison, Megan Peters, Marta Núñez Sarmiento, Victor Tomiczek, Lindsay Uhma, Leonard Vassallo and Manuel E. Yepe, for years of friendship, support and rigorous discussions on life, the universe and everything. For their insightful comments on my manuscript, thanks go to Steve Law, Alice Haspray, Tracey Harris, Nicky Duenkel, Judy Pratt, Kirby Evans and Todd Vassallo. Any errors remaining are my own. And to all the wonderful workers at Navdanya Biodiversity Farm, thanks for your work for our planet and for your wisdom. For being my doorway into Buddhism, transforming my approach to life and being a constant source of inspiration, special thanks goes to my teacher and mentor Ani Pema Chödrön. Many other people have also influenced and supported me on my Buddhist journey and I would like to thank in particular Maryanne Strano, Jikme Chogyal, Catherine Moir, Alice Haspray, Moh Hardin, Todd Vassallo, Josh Clark, Lodrö Sangpo and my friends in the Sydney Sangha and at Gampo Abbey. To my friends Nicky Duenkel and Judy Pratt, thanks for the hours of shared spiritual reflection; in living Tiny, you inspire us all to live large. For their friendship, patience, lots of cups of coffee and just for being good people, I would like to thank my neighbours Wayne and Barb Miller who let me use their basement as an office while writing this book. I would also like to thank the many students who over the years have challenged me, made me laugh at myself, and who have helped me to become a better teacher and person. For their political commitment, efficiency and good will, I would like to thank the publishing team at Zed including Dominic Fagan, Jakob Horstmann, Sara Marchington and particularly Ken Barlow who trusted in my rather unorthodox combination of worldviews. My deepest gratitude goes to my best friend and life partner Garry Leech whose life, work and dogged perseverance on social justice causes has been a constant source of inspiration to me. Without his support this book could not have come into being. Finally, I would like to thank my dear sons Owen and Morgan, who put up with my funny ways and are my greatest teachers.

For Mum

INTRODUCTION

*Even the most brilliant political system can't save the world
if people are committed to a fear-based way of living. Peace
and prosperity come from how we, the citizens of the world,
are working with our minds. By not running from the
vicissitudes of life, by fearlessly opening to them all, we have
the opportunity not only to change our own life but
also to help change the earth.* — Pema Chödrön

*I am not interested in dry economic socialism. We are
fighting against misery, but we are also fighting against
alienation. … Marx was preoccupied both with economic
factors and with their repercussions on the spirit. If
communism isn't interested in this too, it may be a
method of distributing goods, but it will never be a
revolutionary way of life.* — Ernesto 'Che' Guevara

The Dalai Lama has surprised many audiences, particularly in
the United States, by declaring, 'I am Socialist. As far as social
economic theory is concerned, I am a Marxist'.[1] Similarly, on
numerous occasions, he has stated, 'I am a Marxist monk, a
Buddhist Marxist'.[2] Why would the Dalai Lama of all people
say such things? For those of us in North America, identifying

as a socialist has historically brought with it the need to explain yourself (remember Stalin?). Recent events in North America, such as the Bernie Sanders presidential campaign, have softened this knee-jerk reaction and have made clear that, particularly among the youth, there is an openness to at least re-exploring the socialist perspective. Still, identifying yourself as a Buddhist Marxist requires some explanation. And just because the Dalai Lama did it, doesn't mean that average people like me can get away with it! But, like the Dalai Lama, I and many others have been inspired by both Buddhism and Marxism as valuable lenses through which to view our troubled world.

In 2016, Oxfam International reported that around the world the gap between rich and poor is rapidly increasing with economic inequality reaching 'extreme levels'. They report that 62 individuals now have more wealth than the poorest half of the world's population. The richest 1 per cent has more wealth than the rest of the world combined.[3] One poignant example explored by Oxfam is South Africa, where inequality is greater today than it was at the end of apartheid.[4] Oxfam's numbers point to the fact that the 'rags to riches' dream is, for most of the world's population, just that, a dream. Obscene levels of inequality are also reflected in the disproportionate use of the world's resources by wealthy countries. While the Western consumer lifestyle rooted in the growth economy is vigorously promoted around the globe, it is estimated that more than four planets would be required to sustain this lifestyle for everyone in the world. And, as we are rapidly realizing, global warming, environmental degradation and species extinction are the inevitable fallout of our global consumer society run amok.

Meanwhile, the United Nations estimated that one-fifth of the world's population were facing some form of violence or insecurity in 2015. And the number of people forcibly displaced worldwide was a record 60 million, mainly driven by the Syrian war and other ongoing conflicts in the global South. One out of every 122 people worldwide is someone who has been forced to flee their home. Furthermore, there are more than 1.5 billion people living in countries affected by violent conflict, and there is a growing gap between countries that experience relative peace and those living with conflict. As António Guterres, UN High Commissioner for Refugees pointed out, 'Never has there been a greater need for tolerance, compassion and solidarity with people who have lost everything'.[5]

Important world leaders such as the Dalai Lama, the late Nelson Mandela and Pope Francis have all talked about these 'scourges of our times', and a plethora of books by scholars, journalists and activists have been published in recent years that explore the implications of these crises occurring under global capitalism. While scholars and activists around the world are dusting off their copies of Karl Marx's massive tome *Capital*, many other people are being advised by influential voices to at least take a peek at what Marx said about capitalism.[6] As Terry Eagleton notes in response to the idea that Marx is outdated, perhaps 'Marx's "archaic" quality is what makes him still relevant today. He is accused of being outdated by the champions of a capitalism rapidly reverting to Victorian levels of inequality'.[7]

When reflecting upon the poverty, inequality, violence and environmental degradation in our world I (and maybe you because you picked up this book) cannot help but feel a great sense of sadness and fear for the future mixed with a sense of urgency to act. Aware of how pervasive these feelings are in our culture, socially-engaged Buddhists, like the Dalai Lama, encourage us to see that change needs to happen both at an individual and a societal level. This involves understanding the nature of our suffering, or getting the 'right view' of our situation, which can allow us to find hope in the chaos that surrounds us and to contribute to changing the violent and ecologically-destructive structures of our contemporary global capitalist system. It's easy to feel disempowered and to despair, and some days being hopeful can feel like a countercultural, and perhaps even a revolutionary, activity. I will argue that an approach to the world that draws from Marxist and Buddhist ideas is both of these things, and can provide a path out of our suffering.

This book comes from a desire to figure out how we – both as individuals and as communities – can be more effective at ending the violence and greed and environmental destruction that are endemic to the contemporary capitalist system. Drawing from Buddhist and Marxist ideas, I will argue in this book that alienation – from ourselves, from each other, from non-human animals and from nature – is at the root of our contemporary suffering under capitalism. This alienation and the global crisis we find ourselves in, both politically and

ecologically, stems from a failure to understand our fundamental interdependence, or 'interbeing' as Buddhist monk
Thich Nhat Hanh would call it.

Like many contemporary Buddhists and Marxists, I am
motivated by a deep desire to relieve the suffering of our world
– to recognize my own part in both causing suffering and my
potential to help relieve this suffering. To get to the nitty gritty
of how we may think about this question, I will explore Buddhist
and socialist perspectives on alienation, interdependence and
compassion. The goal will be to show how these traditions view
'harm' and, more precisely, how harm is expressed in both our
individual attitudes to the world and through the structural
violence inherent in our economic system. This exploration will
allow us to see how both traditions provide us with concrete ideas
about how to pursue the kind of world we want to live in. Neither
tradition – Buddhism nor Marxism – prescribes a utopian
future society that we should aspire to. Rather, they emphasize
the fact that we need to start from where we are because that is
where we will find the seeds to a more compassionate society,
whatever that might look like. Therefore, this book will focus on
the development of the kind of values that I believe necessary to
realize such an enlightened society.

So while many of us struggle to come to terms with our
personal despair, the inequality and poverty that are built into
our capitalist economic system and the fragility of our planetary
ecosystem make the urgency of taking a stand – now, from
wherever we are – more vital. In this longing to end the suffering
of our time though, we shouldn't assume that ending capitalism

will solve all of humanity's ills, but recognizing that capitalism is the dominant global system and responsible for many of them is an important place to start. This has led me to explore some common 'themes' in Buddhism and Marxism that shed light on why the capitalist system is so destructive to individual human beings, the broader society and the planet itself.

What I will argue in these pages is that the traditions of Marxism and Buddhism are revolutionary as they ask us as individuals and as societies to deeply reflect on our potential as human beings and to act accordingly. Marx reminds us that we all make history, but not in circumstances of our own choosing. In other words, we have to figure out how to make our personal piece of the puzzle meaningful within the lot we've been given and then work collectively to change things for the better. So there is a leap of faith involved, but not faith in the religious sense. It is a faith grounded in a strong belief in what one prominent Buddhist, the Sakyong Mipham Rinpoche, refers to as the worthiness and enlightened potential of both ourselves and human beings in general irrespective of our religious, cultural or ethnic backgrounds.[8]

While the academic in me understands the importance of engaging with the messy debates around the authenticity of particular interpretations of the meaning of Marxism and the various 'socialisms' that have emerged from it, the activist in me is urging an approach here that could be helpful in a more immediate way. Therefore, I will leave the academic debates to the more qualified Marxist and socialist scholars who I would like to acknowledge here as making an invaluable contribution to my worldview. I would also like to confess that the first writings I read of Marx many years ago were the early love letters between him and his future wife Jenny, who was said to be an influence on his political development. Maybe that tells you something about me.

In this book I would also desperately like to avoid caricaturizing such a complex and beautiful tradition as Buddhism but, again, the activist in me says that we shouldn't be silent just because we have not spent an entire life pouring over religious texts with a fine-tooth comb. For many of my secular and academic contemporaries, the idea of drawing on any religion to make political arguments is both anachronistic and possibly very dangerous. I would suggest that this initial response is immanently healthy given what has been justified both historically and in our contemporary world in the name of religion. But Buddhism is not a religion in the Western theistic sense of the term. As such, it could be argued that Buddhism is a philosophy rather than religion (however, this book is not the place to engage in that particular debate). Two great learnings we can take from the Buddha are: not to trust any belief system that we haven't tested ourselves in our own lives; and, no matter how tough things get, there is always a way out of suffering because everything is always changing so there are always new opportunities for cultivating our compassion and wisdom.

But this is not a book about Buddhist philosophy or social theory.[9] The point for our purposes here is that anyone can have access to the radical and revolutionary teachings of the Buddha without buying into the various cultural practices of some of the Buddha's followers. This approach of course will make many people uncomfortable, but luckily Buddhism can also give you some great practical tools to get over that! But joking aside, many books in the popular Buddhist canon begin with a humble apology about lacking credentials, being on the 'journey' to liberation and thus being steeped in confusion and so on. I would place myself right in the middle of that confusion. But, as a good Buddhist, I must trust that the intention I have in writing this book is a good one.

In no way do I claim that the arguments in this book are meant to imply that the Buddhists and socialists whose work I draw from share my perspective or my conclusions. I hope they will forgive me in advance for taking liberties with their ideas. I take full responsibility for my personal interpretations and I certainly do not claim to have an objective reading of these rich and complex traditions. But as an educator, part of my job is pointing out, not only human suffering and its contemporary manifestations under global capitalism, but how to help develop 'ways of seeing' that could assist us in getting out of what eco-philosopher and Buddhist Joanna Macy and her colleague Chris Johnstone call 'the mess we're in'.[10]

Finally, this book is not about the Dalai Lama or Karl Marx *per se,* and I do not pretend to give an exhaustive account of what either of them think or thought. Rather, I am drawing from both the Buddhist and the Marxist traditions to try to explain why a Buddhist like the Dalai Lama, living at the beginning of the twenty-first century, identifies with Marxism (and some of the expressions of socialism that have emerged from this tradition). The Dalai Lama has stated,

Of all the modern economic theories, the economic system of Marxism is founded on moral principles, while capitalism is concerned only with gain and profitability. Marxism is concerned with the distribution of wealth on an equal basis and the equitable utilization of the means of production. It is also concerned with the fate of the working classes – that is the majority – as well as with the fate of those who are underprivileged and in need, and Marxism cares about the victims of minority-imposed exploitation. For those reasons the system appeals to me, and it seems fair … The failure of the regime in the Soviet Union was, for me not the failure of Marxism but the failure of totalitarianism. For this reason I think of myself as half-Marxist, half-Buddhist.[11]

I am not going to argue in this book that we all need to be Buddhist Marxists (phew, you say!). Rather, I will argue that both of these traditions provide insights that I believe, and clearly many others like the Dalai Lama also believe, possess universal value. And I will argue that the universal ideas present in both of these traditions can stimulate hope and motivate us to action to end the rampant suffering caused by the contemporary capitalist system. In reference to how we can make old ideas relevant for new times, Marxist philosopher Slavoj Žižek points out two significant things: We have to 'be true to what is eternal' in them, and we have to reinvent them again and again. So, here goes …

CHAPTER 1

MUCH ADO ABOUT NO-THING

A leaf of grass is no less than the journeywork of the stars.
— Walt Whitman

I first encountered the idea of emptiness as a small child. I was maybe five years old when I looked at my little brother Rick with his mad scientist-looking blond hair going in all directions and wondered, 'Why am I me and you are you?' Which led me to ask, 'How do I know I'm me?' Even at that age, or perhaps, because I was that age, I could sense there wasn't really any tangible or separable 'thing' that was 'me'. Or, if there was, I certainly couldn't find it. A body walked 'me' around, a voice spoke when 'I' wanted to say something, and a tummy grumbled when 'I' was hungry, but where exactly was the 'me'?

Buddhists and other spiritual practitioners have long pondered this question, many meditating for hours, days, even years on it, and seasoned practitioners such as the Dalai Lama keep coming up with nothing, or rather no-thing. Absolutely Nothing or, as many Buddhists would say, emptiness. But we are reminded by Buddhists and physicists alike that it is an emptiness that is teeming with all kinds of life, from sub-atomic particles to entire galaxies, so it is not empty in the Western nihilist sense. It is just empty in that it is, to make up a word, unthingifiable. In other words, it is empty of things that exist in isolation from each other. There is only an interconnected whole and there is no-thing, or no-self, that is not an intricate part of that whole.

But, despite this reality, most of us 'grow up' and the Western socialization process we are subjected to assists in the creation and nurturing of a solid 'me' – what Western psychology would call the 'ego' – which we learn to experience as a thing separate from other things in the world. For Buddhists, this 'me', while we might think it necessary in a practical sense to function in the 'real world', is ultimately a delusion. Albert Einstein agreed. In his words, living one's life *as though* one were separate is, for the individual, 'a kind of optical delusion of his consciousness'.[1]

When we realize that we are not separate (and embody this in the way we live), and we discover that it is in fact *impossible* for us to be separate, we become enlightened or liberated or free depending on what tradition one is speaking from. Zen Master and peace activist Thich Nhat Hanh speaks of the state of 'interbeing', which expresses in his terms what Einstein was trying to say: nothing in the universe has an independent existence.[2] What the Buddhist tradition calls delusion or ignorance is the state of living in contradiction to this basic truth and is ultimately, from the Buddhist standpoint, the source of all our suffering. It is a form of being alienated from our true nature, which is one of interdependence with all things. This

12

alienation is what allows us to hurt ourselves, other humans, non-human animals and nature.

If it is impossible to isolate a thing called the self, and *if* it is also true that all the parts of who we are (thinking, digesting, bleeding, excreting, etc.) are all interdependent, and *if* we are unable to actually exist without nature's air, water, food and so on, then everything that exists is ultimately part of US and we are part of IT. So we, and everything else in the universe, are empty in the sense that we do not have a separate 'is-ness'. But why might this be important to us as individuals at the beginning of the twenty-first century? And how can we understand these ideas in relation to what is happening in our current reality?

While few Buddhists specifically use the language of economics to talk about contemporary forms of alienation (British economist E. F. Schumacher was well ahead of his time),[3] we are increasingly seeing socially-engaged Buddhists such as Thich Nhat Hanh, the Dalai Lama, Sakyong Mipham Rinpoche and Sulak Sivaraksa address the alienation inherent in the culture of capitalism. Sivaraksa, for example, notes, 'Capitalism brainwashes us through advertising and the skewing of priorities to think we need to become someone other than ourselves by rejecting who we are. But we can never become more than ourselves by rejecting who we are'.[4] Sakyong Mipham uses the language of worthiness to argue that at some deep level we have lost our sense of being worthy, both at an individual level and as a broader culture. At an individual level we feel we are too poor, too fat, too old, too slow, too brown, too bald, etc. And if we could just obtain enough money we could fix our problems by purchasing houses, cars, anti-aging make-up, skin and hair dye, diet products, penis lifters, holidays, and so on.

This sense of 'lack', the related sense of low self-esteem, and the instant gratification provided by material things all reinforce individualist, consumerist behaviour, which is the fuel that allows the capitalist system to keep running. And for those too poor to engage in the market, the promise that the capitalist consumer dream may one day become a reality for them is continually reinforced by media and education systems and, in the global South (Latin America, Africa and Asia), by the ideology of the Western development model. But while many of us in the global North (North America and Europe) are sufficiently pacified through consumerism to the point that we accept our alienated state as natural, there remains an underlying sense of persistent unease expressed in the rising figures for drug and alcohol abuse, clinical depression and other 'mental' disorders. Luckily for the rich, who benefit economically from this system, we think it's our own fault because, while we run around feeling shitty about ourselves and wondering where we went wrong, we believe that most other people are living normal and happy lives. But, in actuality, many people are experiencing the same alienation as we are – and depression and other 'disorders' are arguably natural responses.

From different angles both Marxists and socially-engaged Buddhists talk about the ways in which 'value' – including how we value ourselves, others and the planet – is determined under capitalism. Marxists argue that under capitalism all value comes from labour and is realized through exchange of the product of that labour in the market. By selling his or her labour power to the capitalist, the worker loses ownership and control over the product of his or her labour and this disconnectedness from that expression of their inner creativity results in a sense of alienation, a lack of completeness. In short, as Karl Marx noted, the worker lives to satisfy the needs of the capitalist:

> The demand for men necessarily governs the production of men, as with every other commodity. Should supply greatly exceed demand, a section of the workers sinks into beggary or starvation. The worker's existence is thus brought under the same condition as the existence of every other commodity. The worker has become a commodity, and it is a bit of luck for him if he can find a buyer. And the demand on which the life of the worker depends, depends on the whim of the rich and the capitalists.[5]

Under capitalism everything (humans, non-human animals and nature) must be commodified and brought to market in order to gain value. Consequently, aspects of nature such as a flower or a mother's care for her children in the home are not valued unless they can be bought and sold on the market. Only when you sell a flower does it attain value under capitalism. If it remains where it is in nature, it doesn't have value, unless it is growing in a park that people pay to enter. A river has no value until it can be diverted to a dam. Cows have no value until they become steak. Nature ultimately has no value until her various components can be used as 'resources' for consumption. If someone works for a day-care centre, the attention they give to children gains a value because they are selling their labour power and therefore contributing to Gross Domestic Product (GDP), although sadly such important nurturing work is of small economic value in most capitalist societies. But if a person takes care of their own kids, their work ultimately does not have value – hence the refrain 'I'm just a stay at home mum/dad'.

Also, an idea has no value until it is patented. While the idea of protecting 'intellectual property rights' may not be inherently problematic – we should get acknowledgement for and have some control over what happens to our ideas – patenting in the capitalist framework is often used to protect the rights of large companies to make profits at the expense of indigenous and traditional knowledge systems. This is particularly evident in issues such as seed patenting where a small 'innovation' is made to a traditional seed variety and then, when farmers attempt to use the seeds they have used for generations, they face legal battles.

From a Buddhist perspective, this objectification, or thing-ification, of people and nature could be seen as the root of the existential dualism that experiences the self as alienated and sees other people and nature as things to be manipulated. We are alienated because we learn to believe that we don't have value in and of ourselves, therefore we must gain that value from outside conditions (i.e. the capitalist market). Paradoxically, we then support the capitalist structures that maintain these conditions even though these structures and the resulting conditions are often the root cause of our alienation. This state of being inevitably affects our behaviour both individually and collectively, impacting how we interact with our neighbours and how states engage geopolitically.

The individualist and consumerist values that are continually reinforced under capitalism prop-up a dichotomy of greed and scarcity which feeds into systems of structural and physical violence that are rooted in fear. The view is that there may not be enough oil, land or water tomorrow, which means that future-minded states engage in economic and military strategies that have one eye in the present and one eye in the future. But there is always an 'other' that is in the way of what we need. Those others must be pacified, bought, controlled or killed in order to protect what we must convince ourselves is rightfully ours. As Noam Chomsky has pointed out, we believe we have an inalienable right to '*our* resources that happen to be in *their* countries'.[6] Contemporary political struggles from the Middle East to Sub-Saharan Africa and the violence endemic wherever extractive industries operate are just the most visible examples of this problem.

For Buddhists, this violence is only possible because we have understood ourselves as separate and therefore in competition with others, and we have bought into a societal view that causes both our own suffering and the suffering of others. In many ways, this is also true for Marxists, who use the term 'false consciousness' to refer to the ways in which we buy into the ideology of the ruling capitalist class despite the fact that this ideology masks the real causes of alienation and exploitation suffered by most people under capitalism. In a sense, false consciousness speaks to the way in which the ideas of the ruling class become our own ideas without us realizing.

This idea is poignantly illustrated in the 'lucky bastard' scene from Monty Python's *Life of Brian* film where one prisoner of the Roman Empire who is hung up by his arms on the cell wall explains to the 'lucky' newly-arrived prisoner that he may 'get off with crucifixion' for a first offence. To the surprise of the new prisoner, he goes on to explain, 'If we didn't have crucifixion this country would be in a right bloody mess. Nail 'em up I say! Nail some bloody sense into 'em'!'[7] The prisoner's views highlight the degree to which he has accepted as legitimate the beliefs of the very people (i.e. the Romans) who are oppressing him. Marxists highlight the degree to which false consciousness allows the labourer to imagine a better self and a better world, as promised by capitalist elites through advertising and on TV, despite the reality of his or her alienated condition and the entrenched inequalities in society along class, race and gender lines. Therefore, the sense of the 'self' as alienated is a key part of both Buddhist and Marxist frameworks.

Many theorists have linked the breakdown and dislocation of social interactions with the rise of consumer capitalist society. Drawing on academic studies in the mid-1990s, Robert Lane tells us that since the 1960s every generation in so-called advanced and rapidly-advancing capitalist societies has seen a rise in clinical depression with people born after

1945 ten times more likely to suffer from it than those born before that year. We are also, apparently, suffering this ailment at younger and younger ages. Lane points out that this is not the case in so-called less developed countries, suggesting that there's a link between modernity (or the Western development model) and depression that is 'undermining the doctrine that market economies increase well-being'.[8]

It is now well understood that consumerism beyond a certain level no longer fulfils us. Recent studies show that income doesn't correlate with happiness once earnings surpass the amount required to subsist. According to Richard Layard, director of the Well-Being Programme at the London School of Economics, 'Over the last 50 years, living standards in the West have improved enormously but we have become no happier. This shows we should not sacrifice human relationships, which are the main source of happiness, for the sake of economic growth.'[9] So why do we keep chasing after the materialistic dream if it doesn't make us happy? Lane suggests it could be related to our hard-wired sense of scarcity, which is reinforced by our corporate media and by our fear-mongering political leaders. It is also connected to the immediate gratification, or ego soothing, that shopping, like all other addictions, provides us in our desperate attempts to escape our alienated state, hence the phrase 'shopping therapy'. Many of the 'habitual patterns' (as Buddhist nun Pema Chödrön would call them), that are pervasive in our Western societies such as constant busyness, over emphasis on achievement over fulfilment, desire to be constantly entertained and so forth could be seen as reflections of a deeply alienated culture. Buddhist leader Sakyong Mipham goes as far as to suggest that our busyness is often indicative of a form of laziness, an unwillingness to be truly present with ourselves and with others. This alienation is expressed in a general malaise which, as some scholars suggest, is exacerbated rather than solved by our new social media addictions.[10]

Ultimately, how we see ourselves affects every choice we make in our lives, including how we treat others. It is linked to the choices we make in terms of how we live and labour. But where labour is alienated, the 'harm' done is not always directly visible and the worker may exist in conditions where there is no choice but to labour in activities that harm other humans, non-human animals or nature. Indeed, those with power and privilege often depend upon the working-class and the poor to do their 'dirty work' for them. Slaughterhouse workers, pesticide sprayers, mine security personnel, and women who literally carry other peoples' shit on their heads are just a few forms of employment that come to mind. When we look structurally we can see many 'harms', such as the human rights violations in sweatshop factories and the violence and pollution inherent in the large-scale agriculture that feeds Western diet and consumer patterns.

Now while many of us in the global North and some elite sectors in the global South enjoy disproportionate privileges of choice about who we sell our labour power to, what we buy and where we live, this is not true for most of the world's population. An increasing number of the world's workers have no one to sell their labour power to because the global economy does not need them. The United Nations estimates that the percentage of the economically active population in the global South engaged in the informal sector has almost doubled in recent decades from 21 per cent in 1970 to nearly 40 per cent.[11] And Marxist philosopher Slavoj Žižek, in speaking of what economists call the '80-20 rule', points out that due to high-tech advances in production we are moving towards a global reality in which only 20 per cent of the world's labour force will be required to do the necessary work in our economy with the remaining 80 per cent becoming 'irrelevant'. As Žižek points out, 'is not a system which renders 80 per cent of the people irrelevant and useless *itself irrelevant and of no use?*'[12]

So most humans in our capitalist society are alienated from their true self-expression, particularly during their working hours. They are alienated from their own labour (with no meaningful connection to the goods they produce and little space to use their personal skills creatively); they are alienated from others (engaged in competition and/or participating 'together' in alienating work); they are alienated from nature (which is by necessity objectified and commodified under capitalism); and they are alienated from other animals (who are also objectified and commodified). With the emergence of capitalism, explained Marx,

> everything that men had considered as inalienable became an object of exchange, of traffic and could be alienated. This is the time when the very things which till then had been communicated, but never exchanged;

given, but never sold; acquired, but never bought – virtue, love, conviction, knowledge, conscience, etc. – when everything finally passed into commerce.[13]

Consequently, under capitalism, those living in survival conditions are forced, and may even seem grateful, to get paid to do anything: have sex, work at Walmart, pick gold dust out of sewers, break bricks for 18 hours a day, and so on. Whole populations of youth miss out on school in the Democratic Republic of Congo to mine coltan for use in our cell phones while their mothers face systematic rape by government troops and militias fighting to control resources and territory. When we see other people as separate from ourselves, we begin to find ways to justify protecting 'our' resources (such as coltan) – and by extension ourselves – from 'them'. At its most extreme, we use our political ideology or religion to justify the poverty or death experienced by those 'others'. In addition to this, many of us are simply not aware of these interconnections.

Echoing the analysis of Marx's critique of capitalism, contemporary critics have shown how alienation under this system is not only what allows mass violence to occur, it is also at the root of the mass degradation of the environment and the exploitation and commodification of non-human animals. In exploring Marx's idea of alienation from 'human species life', Barbara Noske states,

Alienation from species life bears upon the isolation of humans from their integral relationship with nature (including surrounding nature) and with society. Marx seems to look upon humankind as a whole. For him our species life includes our biology and our ecology (humanity as nature) as well as our potential *to act upon* nature (humanity as culture), and it is this totality in relationships which breaks down in the capitalist process of production.[14]

Noske's key contribution is her persuasive explanation of how Marx's concept of alienation can also be extended to non-human animals who, through the 'animal industrial complex' are alienated from their own bodies and offspring, from the various roles that they would play if not given uniform tasks as part of the production process, from each other because of the disruption of their natural social communities, and from nature as they are raised in cages and warehouses.[15] In fact, Marx's framework of alienation allows us to see the interconnected web of systems that bind humans, non-human animals and nature.

All of the forms of alienation described above depend on systems of education, media and communication to socialize us and reinforce our separateness from other sentient beings and nature. Building on a long tradition of scholars that identify the role of education in capitalist societies, sociologist David Nibert suggests that the content of education is creating an 'indoctrinated, disciplined and docile workforce' that tends to reflect and reinforce what is presented in the mainstream media.[16] He notes that 'the history of women, humans of colour, humans with disabilities, and other devalued groups has been told primarily from the vantage point of the privileged. Even with the current day's increased emphasis on multiculturalism, schools rarely address, or address seriously, the role of capitalism in creating and perpetuating prejudice and social ills'.[17]

We in the global North have to go out of our way to make the connections between our daily lifestyles and the systematic oppression, violence and poverty that exist in most of the world. Thanks to corporate-controlled media and our education systems, these injustices are largely hidden from our daily reality – or are justified in some 'us' verses 'them' narrative. Socialists and anarchists have long pointed to the critical role of the mainstream media, who act as 'agenda setters' playing a particularly powerful role in ensuring that we internalize the dominant values of capitalist elites. In other words, in ensuring that we exist in a state of 'false consciousness'.

As Noam Chomsky has pointed out, this is not the result of a conspiracy. Much of the media are profit-making corporations that are owned and controlled by larger profit-making corporations and, as a result, they have a vested interest in maintaining the capitalist system. It is that simple. In analysing the US media in particular, the Montreal-based Centre for Research on Globalization (CRG) reports that six corporations – General Electric, News Corp., Disney, Viacom, Time Warner and CBS – own and control 90 per cent of the country's mainstream media. Furthermore, General Electric is the twelfth largest US military defence contractor.[18] As communications professor Robert W. McChesney notes, 'The commercial basis of US media has negative implications for the exercise of political democracy: it encourages a weak political culture that makes depoliticization, apathy and selfishness rational choices for the citizenry, and it permits the business and commercial interests that actually rule US society to have inordinate influence over media content'.[19] McChesney points out that the same process of centralization occurred globally during the 1990s, with seven corporations coming to dominate the world's media.[20]

The media functions in capitalist societies by selling advertising, and what determines advertising revenue is the number of readers or viewers. Therefore, in order to attract the greatest number of consumers possible, media outlets tend to pander to the lowest common denominator and to topics that a majority of people can comfortably identify with due to their socialization with capitalist values. Sadly then, as a socialist perspective makes clear, because the corporate-owned mainstream media is compelled to adhere to the profit motive that drives capitalism, it obediently props up the worldview of our leaders and justifies capitalist greed and violence in a way that would make the most egregious censor-seeking dictator envious. With the advent of the Internet we have gained greater access to alternative views but, due to our socialization, most of us at this point do not make the choice to seek them out. And besides, mainstream media outlets still dominate online news search results.

Those of us with privilege and social capital who are not necessarily in positions of power – particularly those who have the good fortune to be born human, white and able-bodied in the global North – can entertain and take care of ourselves in a relatively insulated and controlled social bubble. Every now and then reality pokes holes in the bubble (e.g. the 2008 economic crisis, or some deep thoughts while watching the children's movie *Wall-E*), but the general framework of alienation, reinforced by our media and education systems, has become such a part of our lived experience that we continue to exist in our state of false consciousness. Accordingly, the 'normal' person separates themselves from people who believe differently by labelling those others as radicals, or religious nuts, or uncivilized, or just crazy.

But we are not simply passive recipients in the socialization process; we have the capacity to engage with the dominant ideological views that are being promulgated and, therefore, the ability to challenge them. In the documentary film *The Pervert's Guide to Ideology*, philosopher Slavoj Žižek argues that our values and beliefs result from 'our spontaneous relationship with our social world and how we perceive each meaning'. Therefore, he points out, we have the capacity to question the meaning given to the world around us, but 'to step out of ideology is painful, you must force yourself, it hurts … you must be forced to be free.'[21] It is a painful process that we all must engage in if we are to escape our alienated state. Buddhists such as the Dalai Lama, the Sakyong Mipham Rinpoche and Thich Nhat Hanh echo this perspective by pointing out that we manifest our values in our state of being in the here and now. Often what we manifest as individuals and as broader societies are the internalized values of our alienated culture rather than a spontaneous response to the world around us.

In Buddhist language it is about waking up. As the story of the Buddha's life goes, it was prophesied that he would either follow in his father King Suddhodana's footsteps and become a great leader or he would renounce this life and become a Buddha, an 'enlightened one'. After hearing this, the king, who wanted his son Siddhārtha Gautama to take over the kingdom, was determined that he would be sheltered from the harsh realities of life and would grow up in a world of pleasure and luxury. But at age 29, the young prince ventured out of the protected environment of the palace only to be confronted by old age, illness and death. He also came across an ascetic who had given up all attachments to material comfort in order to devote his life to seeking the cause of human suffering. These experiences of witnessing the suffering that all humans face, and realizing that he may be able to play a role in liberating himself and other beings from this suffering, motivated the prince to seek enlightenment.

Many of us have experiences of being jolted into waking up. Sometimes this leads us to figure out how we can help relieve the suffering in this world. Whether we eat meat from a factory farm, use technology built with child labour or burn oil extracted in conditions of imperialism or war, we are inextricably linked to the suffering of other sentient beings and the degradation of nature. But the reality is that in much of the global North and for the privileged sectors of the global South it is quite easy to eat, work, sleep, shop and live relatively peacefully for an entire lifetime without giving a moment's thought to the reality of most living beings in the world. And it's not because we're all bad people. It's because the threads that tie us to other living beings and nature have been made invisible by our culture of individualism, greed and growth. So while many of us view poverty and violence in other parts of the country or world as sad facts, we do not in any way see ourselves as intimately linked to these other lived realities.

This disconnect exists because we live under the delusion that we are separate, that we are an entity to ourselves, a thing. When this delusion begins to shatter, many of us feel an incredible sense of guilt, shame and pessimism. And when it comes to breaking some of our cultural habits rooted in craving, such as buying lots of stuff to try to feel better, we have our work cut out for us! But while guilt may be where many of us begin our journey to enlightenment, it is not a very productive or particularly motivating mind-set to revel in for long.

Marxists and Buddhists remind us that what could motivate us is reality: our inherent interconnectedness and the possibilities embedded in the present moment. We are connected with all other living beings and nature, and our lives could become richer and more meaningful if we learn to accept and live in this reality. For Buddhists the awakened mind helps to put us in touch with this reality and allows our compassion to emerge. And so we return to where we started: emptiness or nothingness. If there is no 'thing' or being that has an independent existence then the fates of all of us are inextricably linked in an emptiness that is void of 'things' but full of everything. The full realization of this state of interbeing would inevitably lead us to engage with other humans, non-human animals and nature in a compassionate manner. And it is to the theme of compassion that I will turn in the next chapter.

CHAPTER 2

COMPASSION IS A VERB

Compassion is the unfettered yearning that responds to the world with noble heart, the understanding that others are just like us. — Sakyong Mipham Rinpoche

We can think about the kind of compassion that I want to discuss here partly in relation to what it is not: a fuzzy, warm, do-gooder kind of thing. Compassion in the Buddhist tradition is very sharp because it is firmly grounded in a wisdom that cuts through self-centredness. It is about true bravery and, contrary to popular belief, is a lot more exciting than the bravery exhibited by gun-toting Hollywood heroes. It is very practical and no nonsense and, I would even say, revolutionary. And as many Buddhists such as the late Chögyam Trungpa and his son Sakyong Mipham remind us, the tradition of bravery upon which genuine compassion depends transcends the history of all cultures and religions.[1] In this sense, it is universal. It is active. It is strong. It has integrity. The need for its realization speaks not only to the underlying potential of our species but, and not to put too fine a point on it, perhaps to our very survival.

The practical intelligence and bravery underlying this view of compassion is rooted in an awareness of the ways in which we do harm to ourselves, to other beings and to the planet, and the approach has an interesting parallel in Marxist and socialist perspectives. When we begin to understand the ways in which our behaviours cause harm – an awareness we gain from the Buddhist concept of interdependence and from the socialist understanding of how oppression and violence are reproduced through capitalist social and economic structures – we come to see how aggression and violence express themselves both individually and structurally. We will explore below how the key antidote to this situation from the Buddhist perspective is compassion, which similar to its opposite, harm, is expressed both individually and collectively. And we will also see how it is helpful to view the socialist response to structural violence (institutional and social manifestations of harm) as structural compassion, or what I call 'big C compassion'. Any of us that have tried confronting individual or collective harm soon realize that it requires a great deal of bravery and courage. Whether we are speaking up at a family dinner where a racist comment has been made or we are a whistle blower on state secrets, shining a light on harm does not often make us popular. Many Buddhists use the expression 'skillful means' to refer to the tools that we could draw upon to effectively challenge our individual and collective delusions.

Many Western Buddhists and non-Buddhists have been inspired by Chögyam Trungpa's vision of secular enlightenment rooted in the idea of the Shambhala warrior who embodies the skillful means of the compassionate citizen. Based upon Asian legend, the kingdom of Shambhala is believed by some to have existed in the fifth century B.C.E., but it is also understood by many to be a mythical compassionate society led by humble and enlightened rulers. In the West, many of us have heard it referred to as Shangri-La. According to legend, the citizens of Shambhala were highly intelligent and technologically advanced, but it was through what we would today call their 'emotional intelligence' that they managed to create a truly enlightened society. According to the Sakyong Mipham, 'They infused their relationships with kindness and compassion, and they also used them to develop those qualities. This all arose from a communal belief in humanity's inherent wisdom'.[2]

Chögyam Trungpa explains that 'among many Tibetan Buddhist teachers, there has long been a tradition that regards the kingdom of Shambhala, not as an external place, but as the ground or root of wakefulness and sanity that exists as a potential within every human being'.[3] He goes on to say,

> The current state of world affairs is a source of concern to all of us: the threat of nuclear war, widespread poverty and economic instability, social and political chaos, and psychological upheavals of many kinds. The world is in absolute turmoil. The Shambhala teachings are founded on the premise that there is a basic human wisdom that can help to solve the world's problems. This wisdom does not belong to any one culture or religion nor does it come

only from the West or East. Rather, it is a tradition of human warriorship that has existed in many cultures at many times throughout history.[4]

So what does it mean to be a warrior in this regard? Chögyam Trungpa suggests that in the face of all these problems, our heroism must be rooted in kindness. Therefore, Buddhists seek to cultivate the 'four immeasurables': loving kindness, compassion, empathetic joy, and equanimity.[5] They are known as the 'immeasurables', or 'limitless ones', because in the practice of contemplating these characteristics we are directing our minds, and therefore our being, towards an immeasurable number of sentient beings. We could also direct these qualities towards nature understood as a cosmos of living things. This orientation trains us to counter selfishness. According to Chögyam Trungpa, 'Shambhala vision is the opposite of selfishness. When we are afraid of ourselves and afraid of the seeming threat the world presents, then we become extremely selfish. We want to build our own little nests, our own cocoons, so that we can live by ourselves in a secure way'.[6]

The selfishness that Chögyam Trungpa is speaking about is rooted in ego, both individual and societal, and in the 'ME' or 'US' versus 'THEM' mentality. In practical terms, living in *our* cocoons means that we can hide behind *our* social and cultural narratives proclaiming that we have found the ultimate truth in *our* religion, in *our* economic system, or in *our* political system. But to feel secure in our cocoons we must also build narratives about our enemies and fortify ourselves with weapons.

Compassion is the key antidote to this selfishness. Compassion here refers both to something we embody and to what we *do* in the world. But the important thing for our purposes here is that for compassion to mean anything at all, it must entail relationships and action. As Shambhala Buddhist Ethan Nichtern says, 'the practice of interdependence occurs up off our asses'.[7] From this perspective, compassion can be seen as a verb because, when it is truly understood and embodied, it cannot help but transform all the expressions of selfishness that we encounter, both as individuals in our daily lives and as citizens of a capitalist society.

It is difficult to read the news today without despairing at how dominant *our* narrative is in the corporate media's portrayal of global issues. The fact that our world leaders see bombing the 'other' as a key part of the solution to building peace speaks to the completely upside-down view that dominates the thinking of our most prominent ideologues. And many of us support them! Some blindly out of patriotism, others because of misguided ideas about our moral and cultural superiority, and some of us go along with it reluctantly and with some discomfort because we're scared and we really don't know what else to do. Consequently, we live in a world filled with fear, and this fear just happens to be beneficial for many profit-makers under capitalism. Not to imply that these economic elites specifically desire that their wealth be generated from violence (that would be absurd), but if actively pursuing violence (wars), or the inputs to violence (weapons), generates profits and increases the value of stocks then sadly this path is pursued and seen as a rational business decision. The military industrial complex could not exist without our fear, and every war generates increased profits for certain sectors of the economy. It is no coincidence that the five permanent members of the United Nations Security Council, the body responsible for maintaining world peace, are also the world's largest weapons manufacturers.

Given this global reality in which we live, it is helpful for us to understand what a Shambhalian view of bravery means and how it can point us towards cultivating compassion in ourselves and in the world.[8] But in order to achieve this, we need to understand what compassion entails. Compassion in our modern societies is often thought of as something nice but a bit fuzzy conceptually, and not always practical in the 'real' world. It may be appropriate for housewives, community groups, individual philanthropists and churches but there's not really a place for it in the nitty-gritty, dog-eat-dog worlds of politics and economics. But what I want to suggest here is that it is precisely in the spheres of politics and economics – which incidentally can never really be separated – that we need to avoid harm by cultivating compassion. In political and economic discourse, a socialist view would suggest that this could translate into building genuine democratic participation and true accountability into political and economic processes. Having compassion built into the fabric of social relations is something that people such as the Dalai Lama are pointing to when they talk about socialism as a moral system. While this may be expressed differently in different cultural contexts, the backdrop of compassion and of not doing harm, would go a long way to preventing people from 'choosing' fascism. It is our inability to express compassion structurally that has contributed to the rampant, often totally desensitized, violence and corruption that are part of the reality of our current era.

Part of the problem is that in large-scale industrial capitalism, and under corporate globalization, many areas of our political and economic activity that are not compassionate and that do harm are not really visible to us. In order to respond to suffering, even if we don't necessarily see it in front of us, we have to actually know that it is happening. We could go further and suggest that the ways in which our system is not compassionate are hidden from us by our governments, by corporations, by the media and even by our education systems, although not always deliberately by all of the individuals in these institutions.

The fact that most of us don't think about the suffering of farm animals on any regular basis is an example of how suffering is hidden from us. It's not because we don't care about animals, it's because we don't actually see the worst forms of animal abuse that happen daily in factory farms in order to put meat on our plates. Gone are the days of the traditional family farm of rolling hills and green pastures with animals running carefree through the fields and living the good life until they are slaughtered. Most of the meat that North Americans and Europeans eat comes from corporate industrial farming that takes place in huge warehouses that are closed to the public and protected by security cameras and guards. Inside, systematic abuse and torture takes place on a daily basis, and this farming model is plagued by extensive environmental pollution.[9]

In my experience, when people are exposed to this reality, even the most enthusiastic meat-eaters are repulsed by the degree of cruelty inflicted upon our food animals and are truly shocked to discover that livestock production is the single-largest contributor to greenhouse gas emissions globally. So while we might care about individual animals such as our house pets, eating a pork chop for dinner might require us being oblivious to the fact that there is no 'natural' reason that we feel more comfortable sticking our fork into a dead pig than a dead dog and that what we have come to accept as food is socially constructed.[10] By naming our house pets, we humanize them, making it obvious that they are sentient beings, even a part of our family, whereas nameless factory-farmed animals can be comfortably seen as objects. Consequently, we can obliviously enjoy a diet that contributes to the ongoing torture and suffering of pigs and other farm animals.[11]

Because harm and violence are both individual and structural problems, we need to practice their antidote – compassion – both at an individual and societal level. Literally, from its Latin origin, the word compassion means co-suffering or 'to suffer with'. I can understand why this idea might not immediately inspire you. That's because at face value, it doesn't tell us much. And besides, who wants to suffer? Consequently, we are generally more familiar with the sort of compassion represented by giving a Christmas gift-basket to orphaned kids, sponsoring a goat for a poor African family, helping a blind person cross the road, or singing at a home for the elderly. I call this kind of compassion 'small c compassion'. It is easy to identify and we kind of know what to do and even know when to do it. In fact, in some societies we even schedule it for particular times of the year such as Christmas.

While small c compassion is most often driven by a genuine desire to help people and can really provide much-needed assistance that is not forthcoming from other quarters, it can also be rooted in ego, in a view that sees the 'other' as separate. Much of the international aid work, philanthropy and top-down assistance to individuals and communities functions this way (i.e. with the idea that somehow the giver is superior or has/is more than the recipient, or that the recipient should in some way be pitied). Meanwhile, the ethics behind how the wealth was generated in the first place is entirely divorced from the ethics of giving some of it away. This is evident in all of the back-slapping at celebrity events and the 'oohing and aaahing' that happens every time the likes of Bill Gates give money to an African village. Sorry to pick on Bill Gates, I'm sure he's a nice man, but my point is that much philanthropy and charity make evident the contradictions in a society that with one hand generates incredible wealth and power through corporate dominance of markets and then with the other hand 'gives back' a portion of that wealth through charity to help address the massive poverty and inequality caused by that wealth generation. It is akin to breaking a person's legs and then generously donating crutches to them.

Another way that compassion gets expressed in our capitalist culture is through the fundraising that occurs for children and youth programmes, women's centres, cancer research, etc. Again, we can view these as social expressions of small c compassion in that they are part of projects that people engage in on their own terms and at particular times. These efforts, while rooted in very compassionate motivations, take place outside of our regular political decision-making processes in many liberal democratic societies and definitely outside our regular economic activities. So what could be wrong with that? While these actions are not necessarily problematic in and of themselves, they are expressions of a society that has collectively failed to take care of some of its most vulnerable members. They are also reflective of some very strange contradictions that have become so normalized in 'advanced' capitalist societies that we don't even blink an eye at them. For example, we can comfortably benefit from pension plans invested in stocks that increase in value due to labour rights violations and environmental destruction in another country while at the same time attending a fundraising event for local charities that work on reforestation or child poverty. Most of us are oblivious to these contradictions in our daily lives.

Small c compassion in the global North is most often expressed within political contexts where those same recipients are not seen as valuable enough to be cared for at a collective social level; that is, through national policy-making. In a *Globe and Mail* article, columnist Margaret Wente argues that people from the United States are far more compassionate than Canadians or Europeans.[12] She points to the fact that Americans give twice as much of their income to charity than Canadians and far more than that in comparison to Europeans, who she calls 'the world's worst cheapskates'. The Swedes are clearly the worst, only 4 per cent of them give to charity. Wente points out, it is the religious, small-town, family values types in the United States who do most of the giving. She goes on to note that 'while godless liberals talk the talk, churchgoing conservatives walk the walk'.

While Wente expects us to be surprised by this reality, it actually makes perfect sense when we think about small c compassion. Generally speaking, Western Europeans, and Scandinavians in particular, have far less need for charity than do North Americans. Their compassionate values are expressed in more collective, and often socialist, ways that translate into decent social programmes, particularly in the form of good healthcare and, in many cases, free university education. And it is not, as Wente crudely argues, because Europeans sit back expecting the state to take care of every-thing. Europeans willingly pay a greater portion of their hard-earned wages in taxes to ensure that the system takes care of everyone. Traditionally, it has been important to Europeans that they express their compassionate values collectively, that is structurally, through their social programmes and institutions in what could be called big C compassion. In contrast, Wente celebrates the US model in which those people that fall through the cracks in the capitalist system remain at the mercy of charity, or small c compassion; an approach that has never effectively addressed the needs of the marginalized at any point in capitalism's history.

In reference to the more compassionate structures in European societies, US political science professor Kimberly Morgan argues, 'The difference is that their systems consciously strive for those goals and are deliberately designed to ensure broad public access to benefits'.[13] She goes on to point out that even with US President Barack Obama's healthcare reforms,

> the share of the population without health insurance in the United States will remain higher than in any other advanced industrial country ... And the United States does not guarantee the basic rights of paid parental and sick leave – rights assured to most other workers across the industrial world. In essence, Washington's reliance on private social benefits and services – often provided by businesses to their employees rather than by the government to everybody – ensures good coverage for some but poor coverage for others. Those with well-paying jobs usually get the best benefits, and those with low-paying or no jobs get worse ones. As a result, the United States' system of social protection does less to reduce poverty and inequality than that of virtually any other rich democracy.[14]

US journalist Elizabeth Rosenthal, who has been covering international environmental issues for *The New York Times* and the *International Herald Tribune* for several years, argues that the collective values of Europeans are also expressed with regard to the environment. She suggests that this is because in places like Sweden

> such behavior is now simply part of the social contract, like stopping at a stop sign or standing in line to buy a ticket. But more important, perhaps, Europe is constructed in a way that it's pretty easy to live green ... In Europe it is far easier to channel your good intentions into action. And you feel far worse if you don't. If nearly everyone is carrying a plastic bag (as in New York City) you don't feel so bad. But if no one does (as in Dublin) you feel pretty irresponsible.[15]

Rosenthal explains that this isn't because Americans are callous people when it comes to the planet, but rather that 'the U.S. has had the good fortune of developing as an expansive, rich country, with plenty of extra space and cheap energy ... we live in a country with big houses. Big cars. Big commutes. Central Air. Big fridges and separate freezers. Clothes dryers. Disposable razors'. And this culture, she points out, has led to the United States having the highest per capita emissions globally with the US citizen's individual footprint with regard to emissions three times the level in Denmark.[16]

So, at the end of the day, Europeans have done a far better job than North Americans at taking care of their most vulnerable and have been much more environmentally conscious. This reality exists, I would argue, because Europeans have expressed culturally a structural approach to compassion. It is important to note, however, that this approach has not always been translated into foreign policy and international trade. We could argue that the privilege enjoyed by Europeans, like that of their North American counterparts, is dependent on vast global inequalities.[17]

Some people who engage in small c compassion develop a hierarchy of compassion that does not make sense from either a Buddhist or socialist perspective. I once had a discussion with a friend about an organization that was working with drug addicts and sex workers on Vancouver's Downtown Eastside, an area of the city notorious across Canada for drugs, prostitution and violence. The organization created the opportunity for structured, non-violent social time for 'clients' and allowed them to volunteer, thereby contributing both to a sense of belonging and to a feeling of empowerment. While not magic-bullet solutions, these simple acts made a real difference in the lives of the people that I came into contact with. My friend argued that, while we did need to deal with the drug problem in Vancouver, this money was not being well spent given that 'those people' are adults 'choosing' a way of life. He suggested that we should instead focus our resources on children, youth and other people who are actually deserving of them.

This conversation troubled me on various levels. It occurred to me that many of us see a hierarchy of compassion and a clear line in the sand dividing those who 'deserve' it and those who do not. This kind of approach is nurtured in a culture that emphasizes small c compassion: compassion towards 'chosen ones', compassion that we can dabble in when the desire emerges, and compassion that allows the continuation of 'business as usual'. In other words, compassion that does not challenge the status quo or the interests of the rich and powerful in any fundamental way. Again, this is not to denigrate the wonderful people who work tirelessly in our capitalist societies to create safety nets of different sorts for those falling through the inevitable cracks. In fact, the people leading these efforts are often outspoken advocates for structural change, usually running around frantically trying to function with tiny budgets and insufficient time.

The Buddhist view of compassion is quite different from the small c view, and it is complemented by a Marxist framework. While we may determine that we have priorities to focus on at any given time, priorities that we should decide collectively, true compassion does not have an 'on-off' switch. Compassion is not something that we can put on and take off like an article of clothing, nor is there a hierarchy to it. Those who provide medical and humanitarian assistance on the frontlines of war zones to all who are in need regardless of their nationality, religion or political ideology understand this perhaps better than the rest of us.

The Dalai Lama has many stories that illustrate the work, or 'practice', it takes to cultivate this kind of compassion. In one, he tells us of a Tibetan Monk friend who was imprisoned in a Chinese gulag for 18 years. The monk talked about facing 'danger' on a few occasions, but he was not referring to any danger to his life; rather he was concerned with the danger of losing his compassion for the Chinese. Similarly, in a 2014 speech in London on 'Universal Responsibility in the Modern World', the Dalai Lama encouraged his audience to focus their political critiques and protests on the 'behaviours' of individuals and institutions while always remembering that the human beings engaging in those behaviours are not inherently evil and are deserving of compassion.[18]

While this may sound like an idealistic form of compassion, it can have very practical implications. This is evident in Truth and Reconciliation Commissions and in processes of restorative justice where testimony and dialogue between victims and perpetrators can bring about individual and social healing. And while not all of us will reach the heights of compassion and equanimity of the Tibetan monk described above, it becomes clear how working towards this kind of compassion can open our minds to viewing individuals as the product of their environment and social conditioning rather than just in terms of how their behaviour may impact us at an individual and immediate level. For example, it is easy to have compassion for a child living in poverty. It is a little more challenging to feel compassion for the adult homeless person or drug addict who unleashes a stream of profanity at us as we walk down the street. Most of us find it difficult to feel compassion for certain people, but the Dalai Lama would say that is exactly why we need to 'practice', both as individuals and as societies, so that we can nurture these qualities.

While there is no shortage of opportunities to practise compassion in our daily lives, there are also particular institutional arrangements and structures that would better contribute to the development of big C compassion. Not only would all of us benefit from being part of a global society where big C compassion is a guiding principle, but also socially engaged Buddhists would argue that this approach is in alignment with our true nature as interdependent beings. I am speaking here of a much more expansive and existential idea of compassion and one that we will see is, in the Marxist sense, also more structural and societal in that it seeks to ensure the wellbeing of everyone.

An approach rooted in big C compassion, which is inherent in socialism, necessarily becomes politicized in the context of capitalism because it comes into direct confrontation with the structural logic of the accumulation of wealth and the commodification of people, non-human animals and nature. Whereas small c compassion can be practiced within the context of oppressive institutional and social structures, big C compassion, if taken to its logical conclusion, directly challenges these arrangements. Hence why you will not likely be killed for organizing a campaign to raise money for cancer research due to insufficient public funding but you could be shot – and many are – for attempting to protect the collective rights of their communities against corporate ownership and the use of their traditional lands.

So while a socialist concept of compassion implies a structural approach, the Buddhist view complements this by implying that there is no hierarchy of compassion and, because of this, no boundaries or borders that can be justified in promoting the welfare of others. The idea of compassion is a central feature of Buddhist philosophy and practice not because being compassionate is seen as some kind of external ethic to which we 'should' adhere or that we can opt in and out of based on our personal motivations and whims. Compassion is a deep-rooted emotion, or state of mind and heart, that Buddhism suggests we 'uncover' and ultimately embody as we realize our true nature, that of interdependence. It is not a matter of thinking, 'I will learn how to be compassionate' or 'I can be compassionate about this but not about that'. It is a matter of properly understanding our interconnection with all beings and nature – and understanding it beyond the cognitive level.[19] This kind of compassion is entirely without pity or condescension or hierarchy. It is, if you will, a general orientation of our being. When we are genuinely compassionate, we act very horizontally. In other words, while we may have power and wealth, we act without 'power over' and without a desire to achieve some goal of our own that may have little to do with the needs of the recipient. When we take this seriously we will inevitably contribute to building what Sakyong Mipham has called 'an enlightened society'.

So, you say, that's all very well, but it sounds like a rather tall order. After all, I can easily collect donations for the Christmas basket or be nicer to people at work, but what can I really do about the fact that much of our oil comes from Saudi Arabia where they're chopping peoples' heads off on a regular basis? And, even if I try to buy all of my products from fair trade and ethical companies, I'm just one person, so does it really make a difference? Such questions are important, and I will try to answer them by exploring the Buddhist idea of suffering and its connection to compassion.

The Four Noble Truths were the first teaching that the Shakyamuni Buddha gave to his earliest disciples and this teaching lies at the root of all Buddhist philosophy. Buddhism's view of human reality is embodied in this fundamental teaching. The basic idea of the Four Noble Truths is that we all live a conditioned existence (everything we do arises in particular conditions or circumstances and contributes to new conditions) in the world of phenomena (in a world of people and things that appear separate from us) and therefore we feel pain and we suffer. We all experience birth, old age, sickness and death (First Noble Truth). But while pain is inevitable, Buddhists argue that suffering is not. To escape our suffering we have to understand its origin (Second Noble Truth).

Our suffering is rooted in our resistance to the imper-manence and uncertainty of life, which is what Buddhists call 'ego clinging', or what Buddhist nun Pema Chödrön refers to as our 'addiction to ME'.[20] Pema Chödrön has also explained this addiction as an attachment to fixed identity – our own identity or the identity of others – which can lead to fundamentalist behaviour. As she explains, 'The root of these fundamentalist tendencies, these dogmatic tendencies, is a fixed identity – a fixed view we have of ourselves as good or bad, worthy or unworthy, this or that. With a fixed identity, we have to busy ourselves with trying to rearrange reality, because reality doesn't always conform to our view'.[21] Buddhists speak of craving or desire (*tanha*) as an expression of this ego clinging: the things, people, experiences that we continually and sometimes obsessively seek as we try to find secure ground. But as Lama Surya Das reminds us, it is not the things in and of themselves that are the problem, 'It is our attachment and our identification with what we crave that causes suffering'.[22] He goes on to say, 'What the Buddha taught is that we shouldn't try to own each other, nor should we become so identified or attached to anything (person, thought, feeling, career, goal, or material object) that we lose sight of reality – of the relativism and changing nature of all that is'.[23] Once we remove the origin of our suffering (our ego clinging), our suffering will stop (Third Noble Truth). But to do so requires that we follow the 'The Noble Eightfold Path' (Fourth Noble Truth).

The Noble Eightfold Path is essentially a mind/heart journey to end our delusion and to eradicate greed and hatred. It is also known as the 'middle path' or 'middle way' because it eschews the extremes of individual austerity and sensual indulgence, both of which the Buddha himself fully experienced before rejecting them.[24] The Noble Eightfold Path involves striving for and ultimately embodying 'right view', 'right intention', 'right speech', 'right action', 'right livelihood', 'right effort', 'right mindfulness' and 'right concentration'. The word 'right' is not used in a dogmatic sense such as I am RIGHT and you are WRONG, or I am good and you are bad. Rather, the translation would suggest ideas like completion, coherence, wholesomeness and being true in our speech and actions.

The first thing we notice about this path, and the scads of books written about it, is that its purpose is very practical because it encourages us to embody these qualities in the here and now, and this approach reflects the overall orientation of the Buddhist tradition. While study and reflection are incredibly important, at the end of the day it is in our daily being that we express our understanding of these truths. And, while texts, teachers and gurus may be pivotal in guiding us, we have to do the day-to-day work ourselves as individuals, as communities and as societies. In a sense we have to be brave by getting down into the trenches of our own vulnerability and pain and that of others, and getting dirty. But, thankfully, it's all for a good cause: to end suffering.

The first two elements of the path – right view and right intention – reflect the wisdom that we bring to the path; a sense of enlightened awareness that transcends intellectual knowledge. Right intention speaks to the importance of our thoughts. While we often discount our thinking, the Buddha taught that our thoughts are incredibly important not only as the precursors to our actions but because they create 'karma'. Whether or not we believe in karma, the idea that the content of our thoughts and our 'way of thinking' about ourselves and the world is meaningful and has consequences in our lives seems obvious. If, for example, we tend to default to a fearful state of mind, our actions are likely to be more protective and defensive. Similarly, if we generally have a positive view of human nature, we will tend to default to assuming the best of people even in difficult circumstances. Although 'right view' and 'right intention' concern our thinking, the teaching moves us beyond intellectual understanding in that it involves our perception of reality *and* the way we relate and respond to the world differently when we understand that we are not separate, isolated selves living in a world of objects. As Buddhist monk Walpola Rahula explains, this perception is about 'seeing a thing in its true nature, without name and label', in other words, before judgement and separation or 'othering' occurs.[25]

Meanwhile, 'right speech', 'right action' and 'right livelihood' speak to the ethical orientation of our conduct. Rather than being a list of 'dos and don'ts' that can be used to divide the world into sinners and saints, this is where we act in the world with what some Buddhists would call 'skillful awareness'. In other words, as we gain an understanding of our interdependence with others, rather than continuing on auto pilot, we act with intention to remove their suffering. It may be useful here to borrow from the Four Stages of Competency model developed by psychologists in the 1970s. According to that model, we move from 'unconsciously incompetent' to 'consciously incompetent' to 'consciously competent' and, finally, to 'unconsciously competent'. In terms of compassion, this may at first take practice – as we work with 'conscious competence' – but eventually we become 'unconsciously competent', at which point compassion is expressed instinctually rather than as a conscious act.

The final three elements of the path – right effort, right mindfulness and right concentration – reflect the mental work that is required to train ourselves in laying the foundation for, and continually supporting, our path. In simple terms, and as we all know, we have to put some exertion into developing wholesome qualities in ourselves such as generosity or loving kindness and it takes some effort to rid ourselves of anger and greed. Right mindfulness speaks to our ability to be fully aware of the present moment in our body and mind and, in Buddhist thinking, it is also about ridding ourselves of mind patterns that prop up our sense of a separate self. Right concentration is about fully focusing our minds on one object – physical or mental – and is associated with the practice of meditation.

In my understanding, the path is not a linear process, but rather each of the eight elements, which involve particular disciplines, support and build on one another in a more cyclical and constantly reinforcing way. In this sense they are 'interdependent principles'. Underlying the Noble Eightfold Path is the idea of getting our priorities in order for the purpose of ending suffering. Not in the sense of undertaking some sort of moral trip where we beat ourselves or others up for not being virtuous enough, but rather as a path to ending our own suffering and the suffering of others. We arrive at this place through the cultivation of particular traits such as equanimity, compassion and discernment which we practice in the nitty gritty of everyday life. And we can't really develop these traits without understanding our own suffering or the various forms of alienation that cause our suffering. For Buddhists this means that we must understand our own minds, which leads to an understanding of the nature of our being or, as Thich Nhat Hanh would say, our 'interbeing'.

Buddhists believe that the practice of meditation is the foundation that will help to get us there because it is a tried and true way to come to know our own minds. There is much to say about meditation and many ways of doing it. For instance, some people do it to relax, to de-stress, or to deal with emotional and physical pain – and the integration of meditation and mindfulness practices in the health and healing professions has significantly increased in recent years. While these may all be very good reasons to meditate, for Buddhist practitioners there is a more fundamental reason.

Buddhists believe that the practice of meditation can help us to understand how our mind works and to discover our lack of 'self' and the 'emptiness' that reveals our interdependence with all other beings. The inevitable result of these discoveries is that we uncover our compassionate nature. I could write an entire book trying to explain the connection between sitting on a cushion and focusing on your breath for hours and enlightenment, but there already hundreds of books that have been written about how and why to do meditation and the ways it can change our lives.[26] For our purposes here, the point we should take away from the practice of meditation is that understanding our own minds (the way we think, what we think about and how we relate to these thoughts) is essential to understanding how and why we suffer. Other traditions, religious and secular, have their own ideas, perspectives and practices that can help people to understand their own minds and hearts. And we could also expand this idea to understanding forms of collective mind patterns or consciousness expressed in the values of our broader societies and cultures. For example, Marxists encourage us to explore how we have internalized particular values from capitalist culture.

Many of our actions as individuals and social groups contribute to or reinforce suffering, both our own and that of others. Why is this so? If ending suffering were easy and was always fun then maybe more of us would be doing it. In addition to the problem discussed above, in which the suffering we may contribute to is often not visible to us, it is also true that speaking truth to power or acting with compassion in the face of power (which those who try to end suffering are almost always doing) requires a lot of bravery that presupposes a more interdependent view of human beings. As Buddhist scholar David Loy points out, 'the primary challenge for socially-engaged Buddhism is the individual and collective craving for power which, Midas-like, destroys whatever it touches. Power and money may be quite valuable as means to some good end, but they turn destructive when they become ends in themselves'.[27]

At particular points, fighting against destructive expressions of power can mean that we might be disowned by our families, social groups or cultures, or perhaps even that we are killed. We don't have to search very far back in history to find examples of people who were targeted for speaking truth to power such as François-Dominique Toussaint Louverture, Rosa Luxemburg, Emmeline Pankhurst, Emma Goldman, Mohandas K. Gandhi, Ernesto 'Che' Guevara, Martin Luther King Jr., Anna Mae Aquash, Archbishop Oscar Romero and Nelson Mandela. Tragically, there are also many contemporary examples including Honduran indigenous leader and environmental activist Berta Isabel Cáceres Flores who received the prestigious Goldman Environmental Prize in

2015 and was then assassinated in March the following year, during the writing of this book. Cáceres was killed for her work in organizing communities to defend their forests and rivers from the environmentally destructive mega-projects of multinational corporations. All of these people were concerned in some way with creating a world marked by big C compassion.

When we are all wrapped up in our own egos, our 'Me' project – the individualist way of being that is reinforced in capitalist culture – it is particularly difficult, if not impossible, to see the world from a larger and more compassionate perspective, let alone to act in it with this knowledge. When we focus on our individual lives and not on our relationship to others, we become much more concerned with protecting our personal security. Buddhists such as Pema Chödrön argue that our desire to gain ground, to achieve security in a fundamentally insecure world, can lead us to all sorts of deluded behaviours and addictions – individual and societal – and we will go to great lengths to protect our fixed identities and the world views that support them. At a societal level this can lead to horrors such as the Holocaust, nuclear destruction or the seemingly continuous cycle of violence of the so-called war on terror, or it can be expressed in rampant consumerism. David Loy has called the collective expression of the addiction to ME, 'wego', which can be reflected in narratives of race, class, gender and in themes such as religious fundamentalism, patriotism and the capitalist growth economy.[28]

While expressions of a collective identity are not a problem in and of themselves, as societal expressions of compassion make clear, the attachment to identities at the expense of others is where we see 'wego' at work. Any kind of fundamentalism, whether based in religion or political ideology, can be viewed as an expression of wego. The negative aspects of wego are expressed in the idea of harm that we have talked about from both socialist and Buddhist perspectives. We have seen that for Buddhists harm begins the moment we see ourselves as separate from other sentient beings and nature. It is a stance that can lead us to see our fellow human beings and non-human animals as 'others' who can then become the targets of our aggression and violence or who simply become invisible to us. Our compassion in this context becomes conditional. Similarly, for socialists, the commodification and destruction of nature is an expression of this sense of separation. The harm done under the capitalist system results from social and institutional arrangements that benefit a small minority at the expense of the majority.

Buddhist and socialist teachings give us plenty of tools to move beyond the individualist expressions of ego and group expressions of wego as well as their structurally violent consequences. Implicit in these tools is the call to act NOW in whatever roles we find ourselves in to end suffering through compassionate and sometimes revolutionary behaviour. For Buddhists, the way to achieve this becomes obvious when we follow the 'middle way'. Through an exploration of the 'middle way' we can see how the Buddhist idea of interdependence raised earlier can be complimented by Marxist ideas of alienation and structural violence, as we will see in the next chapter.

CHAPTER 3

LIVING IN AN
ALIENATED WORLD

*The most potent weapon in the hands of the oppressor
is the mind of the oppressed.* — Steve Biko

When we begin to take our interdependence seriously, our individual and collective delusions, and the harms resulting from them, become immediately apparent and, for some of us, increasingly unbearable. Buddhism and socialism provide us with useful lenses to first see these delusions and then to actively challenge them. The delusion of separateness identified by Buddhists takes shape in capitalist culture, according to Marxists and socialists, through various expressions of individual and social alienation. We will explore the idea of alienation looking at what this means at the individual level in an individualist culture and then how the social and economic structures we have created under capitalism, which are fundamentally alienating, are the result of conscious human activity which can be both actively challenged and transformed.

While there are numerous interpretations of the Buddha's teachings and different schools within Buddhism, most

Buddhist traditions draw from the *Kaccāyanagotta-sutta*, which deals with the path of the middle way. A key idea in this view is 'dependent origination'. This idea basically gets at the fact that all objects and phenomena (even us human beings) are the result of causes and, therefore, our origin is dependent on something other than our self. As I mentioned previously, Thich Nhat Hanh calls this 'interbeing'. In other words, we cannot 'be' without something else 'being'. In philosophical terms, it is a middle view because it can be distinguished from materialism (and the more extreme philosophy of nihilism or the belief in nothing at all) and from eternalism (the idea of the existence of a Supreme Being independent of causes). And it is because of this approach that some would argue that Buddhism could more appropriately be regarded as a philosophy rather than a religion. In what may be seen as a very Buddhist-style cop out, I personally believe it is both and neither, but I won't get into that debate here.[1] Ultimately, the answer to that question does not affect my arguments.

At this point you might be thinking, 'Yes, but what does it all mean?' The Buddha cleverly avoided the debate about whether human life has meaning or not. This is conveyed in the famous parable about the poisoned arrow, which can be found among the 10,000 or so teachings of the *Sutta Pitaka*, part of the *Tripitaka,* or Pali Canon of Buddhist writings.[2] In the parable, a man is wounded by a poisoned arrow and his family and kinsmen bring a surgeon to him, but every time the surgeon attempts to remove the arrow, the man stops him by asking a stream of questions such as: 'Was the man of warrior,

Brahmin or low caste?'; 'Was he tall, short or of middle height?';
'What was the colour of the man's skin and which village did
he come from?'; 'What was the bow made of? Bamboo, hemp
… and what kind of bird did the feathers come from?'; 'Was
it an ordinary arrow, an iron arrow…?' If he waits to have all
of these questions answered, the parable reminds us, he will
surely die from the wound. The Buddha, being a very practical
chap, advised us to stop getting distracted by metaphysical
discussions and to focus on our immediate situation and our
potential liberation from it. We may imagine him in a Monty
Python-like scene saying, 'Shut up and remove the bloody
arrow you silly fool!'

An interesting parallel for us here is that, in a similar vein
but from a materialist angle, Marx was also not that concerned
with philosophizing about the meaning of existence or the
creation of some future utopia. Like the Buddha, he basically
told us to just get on with it; that is, to deal with the struggles
immediately before us, such as getting rid of the oppression
and suffering in the here and now. As Terry Eagleton points
out, Marx spent most of his life identifying contradictions
and problems in the capitalist system and how we may better
understand them in order to end the suffering and violence
inherent in the system. Very little of Marx's pen time went into
talking about a future society. According to Eagleton, 'The
point for Marx is not to dream of an ideal future, but to resolve
the contradictions in the present which prevent a better future
from coming about'.[3] Perhaps the Marxist version of pulling
the bloody arrow out?

Resolving those contradictions, according to Marx, requires a solid understanding of how economic systems (or 'modes of production' in Marxist lingo) have functioned throughout history and how the related institutional structures give rise to particular social relations. Marx's work in many ways laid the groundwork for the concept of structural violence, although the term wasn't coined until the late 1960s by peace activist and academic Johan Galtung. The approach Marx developed to understand the mechanics of particular economic systems demonstrates how economic structures throughout history have embodied particular forms of violence and suffering and how these structures have benefited some social groups or classes and disadvantaged others.

Garry Leech argues that 'structural violence manifests itself in many ways, but its common theme is the deprivation of peoples' basic needs as a result of existing social structures. Those basic needs include food, healthcare and other resources essential for achieving a healthy existence and the fullest human development possible. Such inequality is rooted in the oppression of one group by another'.[4] Galtung notes that without a specific individual 'perpetrator', structural violence can be much more insidious than direct physical violence: 'There may not be any person who directly harms another person in the structure. The violence is built into the structure and shows up as unequal power and consequently as unequal life chances. Resources are unevenly distributed ... Above all the power to decide over the distribution of resources is unevenly distributed'.[5]

Drawing on an explicitly Marxist framework, Leech extends the concept of structural violence by arguing that the capitalist system constitutes a form of 'structural genocide', which results in the deaths of more than 10 million people annually. Leech bases his argument on a rigorous analysis of case studies from Asia, Latin America and Africa, and data on deaths that can be linked directly and indirectly to the policies and institutions of contemporary capitalism. His analysis draws particularly on policies and activities connected to the International Monetary Fund (IMF), the World Bank, the World Trade Organization (WTO), regional 'free trade' agreements, multinational corporations and powerful nations such as the United States. While his arguments point to the much broader implications of the system in terms of ongoing poverty, deprivation and human rights violations faced by those still living, his immediate aim is to make the political point that the capitalist system is inherently genocidal.

To make the genocide argument, Leech draws on international legal documents from the United Nations Convention on the Prevention and Punishment of the Crime of Genocide, UN General Assembly resolutions and the International Criminal Court (ICC). In his conclusion, he points out,

> While more than 10 million people die annually as a result of capitalism's structural genocide, hundreds of millions more survive on a non-living wage or no wage at all, a lack of basic housing, hunger, sickness and many other social injustices. Furthermore, the structural

violence perpetrated against these people often results in them also being victimized by direct physical violence in the forms of criminal aggression, state repression, social cleansing and even suicide. At the core of this structural genocide is an inequality in power and wealth that ensures the interests of capital are prioritized over those of the majority of human beings and of nature.[6]

Leech's intention is not to suggest that we can take the capitalist system to court or hold it accountable in an *ad hoc* tribunal. Rather, he asks us to think about the fact that a great deal of the violence, death and environmental destruction that we witness daily around the world are not simply unfortunate outcomes of the activities of random global actors and institutions or, in the case of nature, 'acts of God', but are attributable to the conscious activity of human beings functioning according to the profit motive that drives capitalism. And, he argues, the structural genocide clearly cannot be fixed by applying the same genocidal capitalist logic that caused the genocide in the first place.[7]

Even if we don't follow Leech to the genocide conclusion, we should still wonder why so much violence and destruction is allowed to occur on a daily basis under our global economic system, with our consent, and often in the name of 'development' and 'progress'. After all, as eco-socialist Joel Kovel has noted, capitalism is a system built upon and dependent upon 'unceasing accumulation' with a 'grow or die' logic that both historically and in contemporary times has caused huge suffering from violence – both physical and structural.[8] Therefore, we could say that the task of those who want to end suffering is to identify arrows in flesh (a metaphor for direct physical and structural violence) in order to help remove them whenever possible and, perhaps most importantly, to try to stop arrows from being shot in the first place.

To understand why such reflection is important to us as citizens of a twenty-first-century globalized world, we need to return to where we started. Structural violence could be seen as the physical manifestation of a deeply-rooted social alienation. By not recognizing 'interbeing', it becomes very difficult to be truly aware of who we really are, who the 'other' is, and how we are connected to nature, all of which constitute three basic forms of alienation that take particular forms under capitalism. In other words, what links Buddhist emptiness and Marxist alienation is the search for a society based upon compassionate behaviour towards others and sensitivity to the world around us; a world in which we can truly express our true and full potential. The delusion of separateness is highlighted by both traditions, although each uses a very different language to express this reality.

Marxists argue that there are particular forms of alienation that are unique to the capitalist system and that are at the root of much, if not most, of the suffering, oppression, violence and environmental degradation in today's world. So while we don't want to reduce all forms of suffering in the world to capitalism, we have to acknowledge that this is the dominant social system and, therefore, the one we need to be most concerned about.

In many ways, it's the only game in town, and its 'values' have become seen by many as the 'common sense', or natural, way of doing things.

Marx identified several forms of alienation under capitalism and tomes have been written about them. I do not pretend to do justice to this rich literature here. But, like grasping the Four Noble Truths in Buddhism, a rudimentary understanding of the Marxist concept of alienation is useful for comprehending both our own suffering and how we make others suffer.

Alienation is an inevitable fact of living in a stratified and hierarchical society built on a class system. And we can view class here along the lines of Marx's traditional categories of bourgeoisie (owners of the means of production) and proletariat (those who must sell their labour power to survive) to encompass the many layers of social stratification that the capitalist system reinforces. In contemporary lingo, activists speak of class in terms of the 1 per cent and the 99 per cent, the rich and poor, or the haves and have-nots. The point is that massive inequality exists between people both within countries and between countries of the global North and the global South. And, due to the disproportionate influence that capitalist elites have over the world's political systems (including the United Nations), most of the world's population does not have a meaningful voice in the major decisions that affect their lives. Capitalism is, as Marxist philosopher István Mészáros notes, a system of 'structurally enforced inequality'.[9]

While there is no doubt that capitalism has generated unprecedented levels of wealth in the world, Marx reminds us that the generation of this wealth has *always* been rooted in exploitation, thereby creating and reinforcing inequality. After more than three centuries of capitalism as the dominant economic model, half of the world's population lives in poverty and hundreds of millions more struggle daily just to keep their heads above the poverty line. And with the wealthiest 1 per cent of the world's population now owning more wealth than the rest of the world combined, the degree of inequality has gone from being problematic to being truly obscene.

At the close of the twentieth century the United Nations Development Programme (UNDP) highlighted several global inequalities in a way that illustrate the priorities of the global capitalist system. The $8 billion being spent annually on cosmetics in the United States was $2 billion more than the amount required to ensure that all children in the global south received a basic education. Meanwhile, Europeans were spending $11 billion a year on ice cream, $2 billion more than it would have cost to ensure safe drinking water and adequate sanitation for everyone in the global South.[10] In an anecdote that illustrates these absurdities, journalist Palugummi Sainath tells the poignant story of a poor Indian farmer who, when asked what he would like to be when reincarnated in a future life, replied, 'A European cow'.[11] The farmer's response is not as ludicrous as it might sound. Thanks to the massive subsidies provided to agri-businesses in North America and Europe, cows are among the best-fed creatures on the planet.[12]

The inequalities inherent in capitalism and the inevitable collateral damage that ensues – with regard to human and non-human animal rights and health and environmental degradation – is able to occur despite the fact that much of the world, particularly the rich world, is supposedly democratic. The structural violence of capitalism is largely maintained through a separation of the political and economic spheres. Democracy in the Western liberal model does not extend to the economic sphere, and this is no accident. Consequently, capitalism constitutes an authoritarian system because in a liberal democracy the economy remains largely under the control of a small economic elite. According to Marxist Ellen Meiksins Wood, the alienation of power that exists in liberal democracy – through representation in the political sphere and authoritarianism in the economic sphere – is seen as a 'positive good' because it permits 'individualistic human beings to occupy themselves with private concerns. This is why, for liberalism, *representation* is a *solution* not a *problem*'.[13]

According to Leech, a genuine participatory democracy must 'provide everyone with a meaningful voice in all of the major decisions that impact their lives'.[14] This 'meaningful voice' ultimately implies that the key decisions – in both the political and economic spheres – must be made by the population at large through democratic processes that extend from grassroots, or local bodies, to regional and national systems. But under corporate capitalism, most of the major entities in our economic system are not under democratic control, resulting in a huge inequality in power and, by extension, wealth. As a result, Marxists have long argued that democracy must also exist in the economic sphere, which cannot occur under capitalism. Therefore, argues Meiksins Wood, it is not a matter of

> simply tacking 'economic' democracy onto an already existing 'political' democracy. It is not just that democracy at the level of production will require new forms of supporting institutions at other 'levels'. More immediately important is the fact that the political sphere in even the most 'liberal-democratic' capitalist society is itself constructed to maintain – bureaucratically and coercively whenever necessary – the barriers to democracy at the level of production relations.[15]

Given this reality, we should be careful not to confuse things like the Keynesian model with economic democracy, even though it might generate greater equality with regard to access to the necessities of life. While the notion of equality underpins arguments for the welfare state, there has been no move to make our economic decision-makers accountable to the general population, whether we are talking about corporate CEOs or administrators within organizations such as the International Monetary Fund (IMF), the World Bank and the World Trade Organization (WTO). And while the extension of social and economic rights in the second half of the twentieth century through the Keynesian model and the so-called welfare state in the global North was significant and did improve the lives of many people in the wealthier countries, the consensus that these rights are part of citizenship has been systematically eroded since the late 1970s under corporate globalization. Furthermore, many have argued that the welfare state 'compromise' within capitalism did not get at the heart of the injustices inherent in the system. As Leech explains,

> During the Keynesian era, reductions in inequality were achieved within many nations in the global North, but the wealth that was redistributed domestically remained predicated in large part on a neocolonial capitalist system and any nation that dared to challenge the interests of capital quickly incurred the wrath of the United States, as people in Iran, Guatemala, Cuba, Indonesia, Chile and Nicaragua, among others can attest. Also troubling, with regard to the Keynesian model, was its failure to slow capital's onslaught against nature.[16]

Furthermore, the increased equality achieved in wealthy nations during the Keynesian era was based upon the ongoing exploitation of land and labour in the global South. Ultimately then, democracy cannot exist – even only in the political sphere – in one country when that country's power allows it to influence the policies of other countries in an interdependent global economy.

If we take interdependence seriously then, as Buddhists and Marxists would have us do, we would see that, like compassion, it does not end at our borders or with our 'allies'. Very few would deny that our economy is global and, since the late 1970s, the interconnectedness and speed of global interactions has only intensified. Because of this it has become more urgent than ever to acknowledge that our democratic credentials cannot be measured properly within national borders alone, particularly given that so much of our way of life and our wealth and privilege in the global North is gained through global economic activity.

While a Marxist lens on globalization makes this obvious, one doesn't necessarily have to be a Marxist to agree with it. Many people may have a problem with the idea that certain people benefit from the exploitation of land and labour without having to be held accountable for any harm resulting from those actions. And many take issue with the fact that those with lots of money have more democratic rights, or a disproportionate influence over decision-making, than the majority of the world's population. Desiring greater accountability and democracy are not radical ideas. They are actually quite sensible and, despite our behaviour to the contrary, reflect a sense of justice that is deeply rooted in the Western tradition of democracy. The fact that the poor in the global South have no voice in decisions made by the governments of powerful nations, multinational corporations and international institutions that dramatically impact their daily lives can be viewed as a modern-day form of 'taxation without representation'.

While most countries around the world are officially independent, neo-colonialism has ensured the continuation of imperialism in more insidious forms because capitalism ultimately cannot function without authoritarianism and hierarchy existing in the economic sphere. Ask any good capitalist!

Or any worker for that matter. Let's face it, most of us spend the majority of our waking hours as commodities in the workplace, that is until, if we're lucky, we get to retire. In effect, we sell our labour power so that we can eat, drink, have a roof over our heads, educate our children and hopefully stay healthy. Under capitalism, it is virtually impossible to survive any other way.

Most workers have little or no control over how the economic sphere of their lives functions. Very few workplaces in capitalist societies are democratic in any meaningful way, although many people in the public and non-profit sectors work hard to counteract this. In most areas of our economic system, the worker is generally not free to determine his or her path: they have no meaningful say in how many hours they work, how much they get paid, what benefits they receive, or how the product of their labour is utilized – and the consequence of this disempowerment for most workers is a state of alienation. Meanwhile, for many workers, particularly in the global South, human rights violations (long hours, intimidation, blacklists, sexual harassment, and, for more vocal activists, death) are also part of their working reality. In addition to this, there are more slaves today than there has ever been in human history. While figures vary widely, it is estimated that there are between 21 and 30 million slaves globally.[17] This is more than double the total number from the entire transatlantic slave trade that occurred between the sixteenth and eighteenth centuries.

In my own sector, the public university system, we see how even the most privileged of us are in some way alienated from our labour under capitalism. True, this may be 'bourgeois suffering', but it does reflect a broader social problem of how priorities are set within areas instrumental to the socialization process. As socialist journalist Chris Hedges states, 'A culture that does not grasp the vital interplay between morality and power, which mistakes management techniques for wisdom, which fails to understand that the measure of a civilization is its compassion, not its speed or ability to consume, condemns itself to death.'[18]

This is important because, whether we like it or not, university educated people tend to have a disproportionate influence in our society. It is also important because of the critical role that education plays in the development of social values and the socialization of future generations.

But the reality is that, even with all the individual freedom that university professors have in the classroom, they, like everyone else, must work within the mandate of their organizational imperative under the direction of bosses and administrators. And these bosses and administrators must function in a capitalist economic system that is increasingly narrow in focus and crude in its prioritization. In practical terms, under contemporary capitalism, this means that often business, technology and science are privileged over the arts and social sciences, while research that is revenue-generating or industry-connected is privileged over research that is not. This is not because there is anything inherently more valuable in funded research or the disciplines of business, technology and science; rather it is based on very practical and pragmatic concerns in a capitalist society.

The overall corporatization of the higher education sector has much to do with government priorities, particularly fiscal austerity, and the kinds of jobs that students are likely to get under the current conditions of capitalism. In this context, there is an institutional imperative for survival that threatens the more critical role that higher education can play in creatively challenging the dominant cultural narratives that reinforce our state of alienation and separateness. As Professor Nicolaus Mills explains,

> If corporatization meant only that colleges and universities were finding ways to be less wasteful, it would be a welcome turn of events. But an altogether different process is going on, one that has saddled us with a higher-education model that is both expensive to run and difficult to reform as a result of its focus on status, its view of students as customers, and its growing reliance on top-down administration.[19]

A great deal of money is being spent in Canada, for example, on promoting aboriginal business initiatives, and many aboriginal students are being encouraged to study business at university. This approach speaks volumes about a system that does not know how to deal with the historical legacy of genocide and that sees further assimilation as the only way to end poverty and marginalization. Indigenous peoples are subjected to the Western rational enlightenment approach to education that is dominated by reading and writing academic texts. It places little or no value on traditional aboriginal ways of learning, which tend to be primarily oral, and serves an important role in the assimilation process, particularly when the emphasis is on business training. What is ultimately beneficial for Canada's indigenous peoples within the context of the broader society is not something that they themselves have had much space to determine. As Professor Taiaiake Alfred explains,

> Another thing that must be acknowledged is the fact that many of our people are disconnected from the land and unfamiliar with their own Indigenous cultures, and because of this, they hold ideas about identity and their nationhood which reflect colonial attitudes and which have been shaped by the pressures of racism and assimilation. For too many First Nations people, the liberal-democratic capitalist mainstream is the norm and the reference point for their own and their nation's identity. What it is to be Indigenous is largely confused or thought of in terms that are common to members of the settler society.[20]

Similarly, Laura Arndt, strategic director for the Ontario Office of the Provincial Advocate for Children and Youth, points out that the residential school system has left a legacy of distrust towards education in Canada's First Nations communities because it is seen by many as a 'tool of cultural assimilation'. According to Arndt, 'In my house, it is not a proud thing to be a university graduate. It means you're less

Indian because you're educated. Why would children want to get a good education when they feel they lose themselves in the process?'[21]

We don't know how many aboriginal people might still choose business studies if given options with support to study in other disciplines that emphasize indigenous culture and that could prove more fruitful for Canadian society as a whole. For instance, settler society could learn from traditional indigenous approaches and philosophy with regard to decision-making processes, the environment, restorative justice, and health, all of which are inherently oriented towards the recognition of human interdependence and are built upon holistic, compassionate and respectful relationships among people, and towards other species, the Earth, and future generations. This is not to romanticize the indigenous or to deny the infighting and contradictions that exist within particular indigenous communities, but rather to suggest that great benefits could be gained from recognizing and learning from the rich history of indigenous philosophy and practice.

But perhaps more important, and as part of this recognition, Indigenous and African thinkers among other colonized peoples have pointed to the more radical necessity of 'decolonizing' our minds. Ngugi wa Thiong'o argues that the effect of the 'cultural bomb' unleashed by colonization 'is to annihilate a people's belief in their names, in their languages, in their environment, in their heritage of struggle, in their unity, in their capacities and ultimately in themselves'.[22] There are many insidious ways in which our institutions and processes (such as universities in particular and education systems in general) perpetuate this legacy. This returns us to the theme of knowing our own minds both individually and as broader cultures and gaining the 'right view' so that we can end suffering. The decolonizing process is clearly a double transformation in which colonized peoples engage in their own process of reclaiming their cultures and ways of being while settler peoples work to challenge and ultimately destroy the systems and ways of being that perpetuate colonialism in other forms.[23]

Eco-socialism, the spiritual ecology movement and certain approaches used in development projects in the global South are all concrete acknowledgements of the value of indigenous practices and knowledge. In fact, it has long been established that indigenous democratic decision-making processes long predated, and indeed informed, the creation of the US democratic system.[24] Under the Iroquois Confederacy's *Great Law of Peace*, democratic principles were built into the decision-making processes. The six nations were governed by the Grand Council and each nation contained a number of matrilineal clans. The Great Law established equality among all chiefs in the Grand Council. The key job of the Grand Council was to put the peoples' needs first. While men were nominated as chiefs, they were nominated by Clan Mothers who could remove them at any time if they were not seen to be doing their job. Women who were not Clan Mothers could participate in Women's Councils that served an advisory role to the Clan Mothers. The Great Law allowed everyone to voice opinions and all decisions required a consensus.[25]

But it is not only the indigenous peoples' ways of knowing that have been systematically marginalized in our education systems in capitalist societies. And it is not only Canada's indigenous peoples who are being channelled into business and professional studies – these are issues for youth throughout the world. Responsible parents do not encourage their children to study philosophy, especially responsible parents from the global South. Obviously students have to figure out how to earn a living in our world, but the areas where this is possible under capitalism have become narrower and narrower and an individual's value is largely determined by their capacity to generate income and profit in the market. Naturally then, many parents want their children to become business people, doctors or lawyers as opposed to philosophers, artists or musicians. As a society, we are not even aware that, structurally and institutionally, we are making these kinds of choices about what is important, about what values we want to cultivate, and about what kind of world we want to live in.

As a socialist lens makes clear, in many ways, and for many years now, our approach to higher education suggests that we cannot afford to have an education system that does not feed practically into the capitalist economy. The belief that a university should be a place in our society in which we have space to nurture the well-rounded human being has almost become a quaint notion. In our current era of corporate globalization, being able to respond to the demands of the 'market' is the key job of administrators, and marketing the university's 'brand' is the most important role of the development office. Educators increasingly need to prove themselves as 'sustainable' within this context and students need to strategically choose the appropriate professions. This state of affairs does not mean that everyone has made this shift willingly or that nothing good happens at universities anymore, I am speaking here about a general trend. The education system is an important space in which societies should be able to engage in critical discussions about their priorities and directions.

None of the changes discussed above are surprising to Marxists who have long argued that the education system in capitalist societies, not just the higher education system, primarily serves the needs of the broader economic system. Samuel Bowles and Herbert Gintis wrote the ground-breaking work *Schooling in Capitalist America: Educational Reform and the Contradictions of Economic Life* in which they introduce the 'correspondence principle' to demonstrate how the school system mimics the values, processes and structures of the capitalist economic system. Basically they argue that the education system does this by reproducing the inequalities and hierarchies (such as boss/worker and teacher/student) and the values (individualism, self-interest, respect of authority, etc.) of the economic system while creating a disciplined and obedient workforce through the use of such approaches as standardized tests and standardized curriculum.[26]

I would like to provide one example of how commodification of education gets expressed socially. Some might argue that making pharmaceutical drugs is more important to our survival than making music. At first glance, and for those of us not deeply immersed in music, this may seem logical. But a closer look reveals that this is not necessarily always the case, and the question of whether we should make drugs or music really makes no sense outside of a specific context. Research into the effects of music on people suffering from Alzheimer's is a case in point.

In the film *Alive Inside*, filmmaker Michael Rossato-Bennett follows social worker Dan Cohen, founder of the NGO Music and Memory, whose research reveals that listening to music from their pasts not only contributes to patients' incredibly detailed recall of events and people, but it also adds significantly to an overall sense of wellbeing and happiness. There are many factors that play into why this is so, but a key one seems to be the recognition that someone who is old and/or mentally ill is still a person who has a life to live; someone who loves and needs love. The tapping fingers of a seemingly catatonic patient are a particularly poignant part of the story that this research tells. But despite his success, Cohen notes that it is practically impossible to get funding to buy patients even a cheap CD player and headphones so that they can listen to a customized suite of songs. Meanwhile, billions of dollars are spent annually on developing and manufacturing drugs.

The sad reality is that in a capitalist society the most profitable (for big pharma) and efficient (for caretakers and administrators) way to deal with our elderly, our mentally ill and increasingly our youth populations is to pacify them with drugs. This makes them more manageable and their behaviour more predictable, while at the same time allowing pharmaceutical companies to make exorbitant profits. I am not arguing that drugs should not have a place in our society; responsible use of them can be incredibly important to improve peoples' overall quality of life. But the documentary *Alive Inside* reveals how our approach to dementia in particular and the elderly in general constitutes a key structural problem with the healthcare system in capitalist societies. A society that truly recognizes interdependence would also recognize that being old is not about being a 'burden' to the system or simply waiting for death. A compassionate society rooted in an acknowledgement of interdependence would celebrate the contributions of older generations and would recognize that joy and belonging can be experienced at any age, and that all of us will one day be old.

My experiences living in Canada's Arctic and spending a great deal of time in countries of the global South has made clear to me that there are many other cultures, particularly indigenous cultures, that are far superior to the 'advanced' societies of the global North in their attitude towards the elderly. I would argue it is because they demonstrate more socialist values (welfare of the collective, participatory and inclusive decision-making, concern and care for the most vulnerable, etc.) in day-to-day life. Even in communities that have few resources, the contributions of previous generations are constantly acknowledged and the elderly are important and respected participants in decision-making and social life. This reality is confirmed by the 'healthiest place on earth'. The

Japanese island of Okinawa has a disproportionate number of the world's population over 100 years of age. The elderly on this island, even those in their 90s and early 100s, are incredibly active, engaging in many activities such as martial arts, farming and fishing. While a warm climate and a mostly plant-based diet are determined to be significant factors, ongoing active involvement in the community seems to be key in their continuing zest for life, which is truly inspiring.[27]

Education and our approach to the elderly are just two areas where we see the driving logic of capitalism extinguishing the potential of more holistic and compassionate approaches rooted in an acknowledgement of interdependence. But capitalism does not drive itself. It could not exist without us daily, willingly, engaging with it. And we engage with capitalism for the most part without thinking about it, not only because we were born into this system and it just seems 'normal', but also because capitalism taps into the deep sense of lack and fear that permeate our culture.

What is perhaps most disconcerting is that many of us haven't even noticed these trends occurring. And the more alienated we become, the less likely we are to realize that more and more areas of our lives are being colonized by the instrumental rationality of capitalism. As we become disconnected, or alienated, from our true selves, we also become incapable as societies of recognizing the directions that we're moving in and of questioning whether or not we want to go in those particular directions. This alienation is inevitable under capitalism in the view of, not only Marxists, but also many socially-engaged Buddhists. The social, political and economic structures created under capitalism result in a deeply alienated culture that, in its denial of interdependence, promotes and justifies social hierarchies and the use and abuse of people, non-human animals and nature.

Creating a more compassionate world and ending the inequalities that exist in the capitalist system would require us taking a radically different approach to social organization, one that recognizes our shared humanity and the equal right we all have to a voice in the major decisions that affect our lives. But to initiate such as societal shift we first need to recognize the damage being done to us all by the capitalist system in order to begin the process of alleviating our suffering. In other words, in order to begin pulling out arrows.

CHAPTER 4

CONSUMER CITIZENS IN A GLOBALIZED SOCIETY

Overcoming poverty is not a task of charity, it is an act of
justice. Like Slavery and Apartheid, poverty is not natural.
It is man-made and it can be overcome and eradicated by
the actions of human beings. — Nelson Mandela

My nine-year-old son Owen, who is often seen carefully moving small bugs from the house or driveway to somewhere safer and greener, pondered aloud recently, 'Do you think Mother Nature created human beings as a kind of joke?' Then, after some reflections on how human beings are part of nature, he started to pretend to punch himself while saying, 'Let's see how fast Mother Nature can destroy herself'. This little episode led to a long conversation between us about cause and effect and whether human beings are innately destructive and bad. It also led to much serious reflection on my part about how children today are growing up to understand humanity and their relationship to the planet.

A 2010 study of toddlers ages three to five conducted by researchers at the University of Madison-Wisconsin and the

University of Michigan concluded that the children could identify one thousand corporate brands but less than ten native plants and animals. One of the lead researchers of the study pointed out, 'Children as young as three are feeling social pressure and understand that consumption of certain brands can help them through life'.[1] Could there be a more poignant example of the false consciousness and alienation expressed in Buddhist and Marxist philosophy?

At the same time, scientists are telling us that we are currently in the sixth mass extinction period of plants and animals in the last half billion years. They say that while past mass extinctions were caused by natural shifts in climate, asteroid strikes and volcanoes, the current extinction is almost entirely caused by human beings. This is quite a dubious achievement. Some species extinctions occur as part of natural processes at what is called a natural 'background rate' of one to five species per year. But scientists estimate that we are currently losing species at 1,000 to 10,000 times the natural background rate with dozens of species going extinct every day.[2] As the late scientist and activist Peter Warshall reflected,

> From the point of view of non-human nature, this is the Dis-Information Age: the information contained in genes of species is being lost faster than ever and cannot be replaced. No available information from politicians or philosophers seems to be very effective in helping maintain the planet's genetic library. ... This century will be known for its Species Holocaust.[3]

This is most starkly evident in the fact that humans are currently destroying the Amazon Rainforest at a rate of one football field per minute, mainly for livestock production to feed markets in the global North and China. While greed and destructiveness are not new to our species, a Marxist view of our recent history points to the fact that under capitalism we seem to have opened the zip file. Mass industrial production and the commodification of all living things, including the very seeds of life, has ensured that we are now in the position of possibly causing our own extinction. And, from a child's perspective, it appears quite absurd and even masochistic. Children haven't learned yet to explain it all away with economic theory or to write it off as human nature or as 'just the way the world is'. Thank the universe for that! Every time I begin to feel pessimistic, I look at my children, or any children, and try to remind myself that pessimism is a luxury we can ill afford.

Indigenous peoples and the deep ecology movement, both of which I would argue reflect many of the socialist and Buddhist values I discuss in this book, remind us that there is a long view of time, one that recognizes our interconnectedness by asking us to live with past and future generations in heart and mind. The age of immediacy, speed and information overload has led us to a very narrow focus.[4] In this narrowing of focus we have become alienated from ourselves, from our fellow human beings, from other animals, from nature and from future generations. And because of this we are suffering. As Leech points out, in the global North part of this suffering comes from denial:

The belief that we can achieve sustainable development in wealthy nations such as the United States and Canada without dramatically diminishing our levels of material comfort is a form of denial that suggests we can have our cake and eat it too. Such denial is not surprising. After all, the idea of dramatically reducing our material consumption to achieve sustainable development is anathema both to corporations and to consumers who have been indoctrinated to associate success and happiness with material wealth ... Capitalism requires a constantly expanding production and consumption of goods, which can only be achieved through the increased exploitation of the planet's natural resources at an unsustainable rate.[5]

If, as Leech and other socialists have argued, this destructive process is due to the inherent logic of capitalism, what is to be done? As I suggested previously, Marxists and Buddhists share the notion that alienation is at the root of human suffering. And, as I also noted, both approaches are very present-focused rather than future-oriented in the sense that they are less concerned with drawing up a blueprint for a future utopian society and more concerned with ending the conditions of suffering that exist in the world today. This focus on acting in the present in order to end delusion, greed and hatred is based on the belief that by acting *now* in compassionate ways we will automatically contribute to building a new society. So, explaining and ending suffering, we could say, is the whole point of both traditions. Liberation from oppression and attaining enlightenment are the goals.

The adherents of some of the perspectives that I highlight in this book, and particularly in this chapter, come from the deep ecology, indigenous and localization movements and would not necessarily self-identify as socialist or Buddhist. But I point to them for two reasons: one is the belief that the 'eternal' values that Buddhism and socialism together express find parallels in many important contemporary social movements; and secondly, that one need not identify specifically with Buddhism or socialism to hold similar views and to be a conscientious global citizen. The point is, rather, that Buddhism and socialism provide us with an extremely helpful and expansive way of understanding ourselves and others in the contemporary world, an understanding that may also open us up to working in solidarity with others who come from a similar standpoint.

In this exploration we have to first understand the nature of our suffering in order to actually alleviate or eradicate it. In fact, misreading the roots of our suffering is one of our greatest problems as human beings. In this sense, the story that we tell ourselves about our suffering is incredibly important. What I have argued up to now is that the frameworks provided by Buddhists and Marxists could be both inspiring and very helpful to us in our journey to end human suffering. The fact that individual Buddhists and Marxists, as well as Buddhist and Marxist movements, have also contributed to suffering cannot be denied.[6] In this exploration we make a separation between the core ideas of these traditions and some of their institutionalized manifestations. The idea is to draw on some ideas in each of these traditions that point to ways in which we can connect our conscious daily activity to broader social shifts and the transformation of our society towards something more sane and compassionate. There are two connected levels on which this transformation needs to occur. One relates to our sense of self and the other to how we identify with the dominant messages (or what some would call ideology) of our society.

In capitalist societies we are led to believe that most of our suffering comes from not being or having enough. This story is so pervasive that even if we have spent most of our lives rejecting it intellectually, we can still *feel* like we're less than we should be. And the message is reinforced by the media, our education system and the constant barrage of advertising that we encounter daily. As part of my Buddhist practice, I have attended many workshops and retreats in which participants are asked to reflect on the question: Do you feel that you are basically good? The response is not supposed to be dictated by theory or some 'objective' notion of good and bad. Nor is it supposed to reflect how one thinks others see them. The response is supposed to be based on whether you *feel* you are a good person. Most people seem to really struggle with this question, with some breaking into tears because they are shocked to discover that deep down they have a very negative view of themselves.

Many Asian Buddhist teachers have noted that the idea that humans are basically bad seems particularly dominant in the West. As Sakyong Mipham points out, 'When I am teaching in the West, people talk about self-loathing and self-aggression'.[7]

He believes this negative self-perception comes from a deep sense of unworthiness and a 'skepticism about human nature'.[8] While there are various perspectives on why this may be so, some scholars have argued that traditional Christian views of the notion of 'original sin' may play a role in this negative sense of self by implying a built-in guilt and condemnation with regard to human responsibility.[9] In contrast, in Asian philosophy and religion, the idea of basic goodness has a long history. Tibetan master Chögyam Trungpa developed a secular programme of teachings around this idea for a Western audience. 'Goodness' in this vein is not about good versus bad but rather the notion that our fundamental or primordial 'isness' is beyond any judgement of good or bad. As with everything in the natural world, who we are fundamentally transcends good or bad. We are not a mistake; there is no original sin that we have committed.

According to Buddhist teachers, how we feel about ourselves is incredibly important. It permeates everything from our consumer choices to whether we care about how our behaviour could be affecting other beings and nature. As I mentioned earlier, Sakyong Mipham, leader of the Shambhala movement in North America, explains this in terms of the idea of worthiness.[10] When we do not see ourselves as worthy, we will engage in many behaviours that undermine our wellbeing and often the wellbeing of others. This notion extends to our feelings of social and cultural worthiness. If we do not feel that our society or culture is worthy, we won't make the effort to help it. On the other hand, if we think our culture is the *only* one that is worthy, we have also missed the point. This latter view can be expressed in racism, patriotism and often in the violence of warfare. So, for Buddhists, it is very important that we realize our worthiness and, ultimately, that we understand our interdependence. With such an understanding, our caring would inevitably extend far beyond our families and loved ones to embrace all sentient beings and the natural world. So how do we come to understand our interdependence and how does this connect to the idea of suffering?

Returning to the Noble Eightfold Path, while the trajectory of the path is not exactly linear, it is helpful to acknowledge at the outset that having the 'right view' is like having a foundation to which we can always return. And you will remember that we are not talking about right versus wrong in the moral sense, but rather about a more holistic view and being more true in our feelings, thoughts, speech and actions. A big part of this, as mentioned previously, is getting the story of our worthiness straight and, in effect, having the concrete intention not to cause harm to ourselves or others. When we gain a proper sense of our interdependence, everything else – our intentions, speech, actions, livelihood, effort, mindfulness and concentration – will be directed towards embodying this reality in our hearts and minds.

I will focus here on 'right view' and 'right livelihood', but it is with the belief that neither of these truths have integrity without 'right intention', 'right speech' and 'right action', or without 'right effort', 'right mindfulness' or 'right concentration'. A focus on 'right view' allows us to reflect on the connections between our experience of alienation under capitalism in particular, and within the broader social structures that we exist in. The focus on 'right livelihood' provides us with a window into understanding the incredible importance of our individual and societal choices and about how we work and how we produce in the world.

For Marxists, our sense of self is intimately connected to the particular economic system that we live under. How we labour – what we 'do' as work, and how we interact with the rules of this economic system – speaks to more than our life choices (or lack thereof) with regard to jobs. In our daily actions and work we are, through our conscious activity, making choices (either actively or passively) to support or resist a particular view of the world. In other words, what we 'do' every day, particularly in our work because this is where we spend most of our time, becomes an expression of who we are. Both Marxists and Buddhists emphasize this dialectic of *being* and *doing*. Marx said we make history, but not in circumstances of our own choosing. So while we were born into capitalism, we are not stuck with it. We have the opportunity to change our lives and society through our daily activities. Buddhists also believe this. Sakyong Mipham says that we are creating society everyday whether we consciously make a choice about that or not. He of course argues that to allow a more enlightened society to emerge, we need to wake up to that fact and take responsibility for what we are choosing – for our own sakes and for the sake of future generations.[11]

So, in other words, living on auto pilot means that we are by default supporting the existing structures of our society.

If at some subconscious level we feel this is problematic, we might experience depression and anxiety and will often try to cope with the contradictions by engaging in all kinds of destructive behaviour, or what Pema Chödrön calls 'habitual patterns'. These patterns are expressed in both individual and societal choices that often lead to massive suffering. At the individual level we may be addicted to alcohol, TV, social media or video games, while as a society we are highly addicted to consumerism. Furthermore, we are often deeply wed to the practices and views that cause our suffering, sometimes defending those views and practices to the death. We feel compelled to tell ourselves a story that allows us to remain oblivious because, as Slavoj Žižek points out, gaining our freedom can be painful.

The Buddhist view implies that acknowledging inter-dependence in our being and doing is what gives birth to this freedom. It opens our eyes to the suffering we cause ourselves and others but also, thankfully, it shows us a way out. However, getting there may involve a shattering of everything we hold to be true (i.e. ego, wego, fixed identities, etc.) and that can be bloody painful! While Marxists speak of false consciousness, Buddhists speak of delusion. Both are part of the broader picture of individual and collective alienation that I discussed earlier and are, by necessity, intimately connected to the dominant structures and views of our society. Social structures are ultimately made and reinforced by the conscious activity of living human beings. That is both the bad news and the good news. We make the messes and fire the arrows, but we are also capable of cleaning up the messes, not shooting the arrows, and healing the wounds.

One big mess that we need to clean up is the capitalist system, which determines how we produce and consume. While we can acknowledge that capitalism takes many forms around the world, Marxists and other critics of capitalism have argued that there is an inherent logic in the system that is both inescapable and ultimately destructive.[12] Understanding this logic allows us to get at uncomfortable truths related to what E. F. Schumacher called 'the problem of production'.

In his 1973 book *Small is Beautiful,* Schumacher warned about the dangers of the belief held in the West that the essential features of the production system – advanced technology and large-scale industry – had been figured out and all that remained was to transfer the education and technology in order to get the rest of the world up to speed. The 25th anniversary edition of this ground-breaking book was published in 1999 and it included commentaries from contemporary environmentalists, economists, energy policy analysts, indigenous activists and philosophers who pointed out how the almost religious belief in the growth-at-all-costs economy still dominates.

With an eye to bringing more sanity and compassion to our economic system, Schumacher coined the term 'Buddhist economics' in 1955 while working as an economic consultant in Burma. Schumacher's friend and colleague George McRobie tells of a conversation with Schumacher a week before his death where he spoke of the need to apply the ideas of intermediate technology – putting people and environment first and grounding projects in the local – in the global North instead of focusing on 'helping' the so-called developing world to 'catch up' with us and our large-scale unsustainable system. According to McRobie, 'We need to ask of technology, and of any economic activity: Is it good for people? Is it good for the environment? Is it good for the resource base? These are the three questions that Schumacher basically was asking'.[13] Foreshadowing the insights of my son decades later, Schumacher noted the destructiveness of the capitalist growth economy, 'Modern man does not experience himself as part of nature but as an outside force destined to dominate and conquer it. He even talks of a battle with nature, forgetting that, if he won the battle, he would find himself on the losing side'.[14]

But let's try not to get too distressed by the thought that Schumacher's message was delivered over four decades ago and it seems that the world is still not listening. In actuality, increasing numbers of us are listening and many people around the world are working hard to create alternatives both in theory and practice. But the sad fact is that we're no closer systemically to tackling the ethical and environmental implications of our capitalist production system and the forms of alienation and violence that emerge from it. If anything, as the massive expansion of consumerism in China, India and the former Soviet Union attest, this view of, and path to, 'development' resemble a runaway train. And as Schumacher pointed out, this is because the 'view' that we're essentially on the right path is still 'held by virtually all the experts, the captains of industry, the economic managers in the governments of the world, the academic and not-so-academic economists, not to mention the economic journalists'.[15] And as long as those folks dominate the system and its channels of communication (and socialization), many of us will passively accept this view.

We in the so-called advanced countries occasionally wonder why there is so much poverty, violence and protest in the global South because we don't see any of this reality as connected to our own lives. But as we gain an understanding of how structural violence works – that it is harm caused by institutional social arrangements that benefit us at the expense of others – it becomes more obvious why these conditions exist in the global South. Through this lens, we may even begin to look at our fellow global citizens in the countries called 'Third World' – and 'Fourth World', which refers to subpopulations such as the indigenous in the 'First World' who live in Third World conditions – as the primary victims of our economic system. This is why, under conditions of economic globalization, the 'right view' is by necessity global and structural. In other words, it understands how economic and social institutions embody particular practices and worldviews that ensure the continuation of the system.

With this in mind it becomes important to understand how alienation gets expressed in the form of structural violence and how it manifests in our political, educational and media systems. As I mentioned before, Marxists and socially-engaged Buddhists, though from different angles, make essentially the same point regarding our interdependence, suggesting that alienation is a core negative consequence of capitalism:

alienation from ourselves, our fellow human beings, non-human animals and nature.[16] These two approaches come together when we talk about consumerism and the related problem of production. It is important here to distinguish consumerism from consumption, given that humans will always need to consume a certain amount of nature's resources in order to survive. The problem with capitalist consumerism is that consumption far beyond what we need to survive has become the defining feature of our social lives. In fact, it has reached the point that our role as consumers is viewed as more significant than our role as citizens. And this role conveniently distracts us from more pressing questions.

Nowhere was this illustrated more poignantly than in the United States in the aftermath of the 9/11 attacks when President George W. Bush advised people to respond by going shopping and by visiting Disney World. In other words, rather than do things like spend time at home with family and friends, reach out to people in their communities, focus on what really matters in life or what is actually happening in the world, he advised Americans to continue with their consumerist lifestyle and, in fact, to celebrate it. In other words, to further entrench their alienation. In an article in the *Washington Post*, professor of history and international relations, Andrew Bacevich, pointed out that the bill for this 'credit-fuelled consumer binge' came in with the 2008 economic crisis and a protracted war in the Middle East.[17] The Bush administration, he argues, wanted the public to remain passively supportive of its expansionist goals in the Middle East:

The central purpose was to secure U.S. preeminence across the strategically critical and unstable greater Middle East. Securing preeminence didn't necessarily imply conquering and occupying this vast region, but it did require changing it – comprehensively and irrevocably. This was not some fantasy nursed by neoconservatives at the Weekly Standard or the American Enterprise Institute. Rather, it was the central pillar of the misnamed enterprise that we persist in calling the 'global war on terror'.[18]

Speaking at a Pentagon press conference shortly after 9/11, Secretary of Defence Donald H. Rumsfeld made US priorities quite clear, 'We have a choice, either to change the way we live, which is unacceptable, or to change the way that they live, and we chose the latter'.[19] This statement was perfectly in line with those made previously by President Bush making it clear that the American way of life (i.e. capitalist consumerism) would not be compromised. Early in his presidency, Barack Obama was adamant that he also intended to continue in this tradition when he declared, 'Just like the 20th century, the 21st century is going to be another great American century ... we will never apologize for our way of life, we will never waiver in its defense ... The United States has been and will remain the one indispensable nation in world affairs'.[20] But while we are busily engaged in our consumer lifestyles, much is going on that we should be concerned about: poverty, worsening inequality, environmental degradation and seemingly endless wars to protect 'our way of life'.

Meanwhile, our consumer habits are also of great interest to those in the corporate world who use technology and social media to ensure that we can be efficiently and effectively monitored on an ongoing basis. The consumerist lifestyle and how we relate to our 'things' is intimately linked to systems of authority, surveillance and social control. In a talk on corporatization of the media, Indian journalist P. Sainath noted that people are under more surveillance today than ever before. The key difference is that we are not only being monitored by governments but also by corporations, whether through our 'points' cards at store checkouts or through the websites we visit. Furthermore, notes Sainath, the information that is routinely gathered from us by corporations is shared with government agencies such as the Department of Homeland Security, the CIA, the FBI, MI5 and the like. In other words, as a socialist lens reveals, it is not only our labour power, but also our behaviour as consumers (where we spend our hard-earned cash and what we spend it on) that is, in the capitalist view, the most important thing about us.[21]

All of this consumerism might not be so problematic if we were actually fulfilled by it and were not harming ourselves, others and the planet. As I noted previously, the problem is not that we consume *per se*, but rather that those of us with sufficient wealth are engaged in rampant consumerism which, as Marxists remind us, requires a production system that, by necessity, cannot be bothered with questions related to the environment or the rights of living beings. It is not that power-holders in the capitalist system enjoy causing suffering to others and nature, it's just that the logic of capital accumulation requires that these consequences of their profit-making remain secondary considerations. Therefore, a 'right view' requires a questioning of the logic of the growth model and a serious critique of consumerism.

Furthermore, at a psychological level, alienation is a core motivation for our consumption habits. When our buying is motivated by a sense of lack about ourselves and our lives (or as Shambhala Buddhists would say, a feeling that we are not good enough or that we made some kind of mistake); or a desire to keep up with the Joneses; or to constantly obtain the newest, latest version of everything on a continual basis, we can begin to see the behaviour as a form of neurosis. We only have to look to the research on depression and anxiety in North America to see that we have not become happier with mass consumption. As mentioned previously, the explosion of consumerism since the 1950s has not increased our levels of happiness. And for some, the ailments go far beyond everyday neuroses. In his book, *Heroes: Mass Murder and Suicide*, Italian Marxist Franco 'Bifo' Berardi argues, 'An epidemic of unhappiness is spreading across the planet while capital absolutism is asserting its right to unfettered control of our lives'.[22] Berardi draws from World Health Organization (WHO) statistics that show worldwide suicides have increased by 60 per cent in the last 45 years and there has apparently been a 'remarkable increase' of suicides among the young in particular.

While happiness, a slippery concept at best, should not necessarily be the only measure of a good society, it is likely that most people worldwide would consider it an important one. The Dalai Lama has said on many occasions that it is perfectly logical, and not inherently problematic, that all human beings seek to pursue happiness and to avoid suffering. Therefore, the pertinent questions are: What does our happiness consist of? And in what ways can we pursue our happiness without harming others or nature? The pioneering work of education professor Catherine O'Brien is instructive in this regard. Her concept of 'sustainable happiness' is used to describe a 'Happiness that contributes to individual, community and/or global wellbeing and does not exploit other people, the environment, or future generations'.[23] Clearly, as socially-engaged Buddhists remind us, it is not only the negative personal motivations that drive us to over-consume that should concern us, but also the fact that our consumerism causes so much harm and violence to other beings and is ecologically destructive. It's one thing to harm one's self; it is quite another thing to harm others or to destroy the capacity of future generations to meet their needs.

The fact that we constantly feel we need more to feel better is expressed personally in our individual consumer desires and choices, and structurally and culturally in our belief in the growth economy. In referencing the Buddha's three root causes of evil – greed, hatred and ignorance – Sulak Sivaraksa, twice-nominated for the Nobel Peace Prize and a founding member of the International Network of Engaged Buddhists, explains, 'Today, the dominant form of greed is consumerism; we try to overcome the emptiness of our lives by increased consuming. We are at the mercy of advertisers, and, inevitably, we are exploited. The lust for power, a form of hatred, can lure us to defend unjust social systems'.[24] He goes on to argue that, as long as we remain focused on training people to become employees in the exploitative structures of the capitalist system, and allow television and video games to be the primary instillers of values in our children, ignorance will prevail and critical consciousness will not emerge.

Author, filmmaker and activist Helena Norberg-Hodge, a pioneer of the 'New Economy Movement' and winner of the Right Livelihood Award in 1986, has been researching the impact of the global capitalist economy on cultures and agriculture around the world for the past thirty years.[25] As part of the New Economy Movement, which emphasizes 'localization' – grassroots democratic management of economic projects and sustainable use of local resources – she and many others argue that the health and wellbeing of people and the planet should be prioritized over economic growth. These ideas are expressed in her articulation of the 'Counter Development Movement', which seeks to promote autonomous, self-reliant and ecologically-sound communities.[26] According to Norberg-Hodge, by applying 'counter development' in the First World, we could 'heal ourselves and the planet'. To do this,

> we need to regain control of these levers [Regulation, Taxes and Subsidies, and Measures of Societal Well-being] through economic activism, underpinned by an understanding of the workings of globalization. If the

multitude of social and environmental movements link hands to address a common agenda, sufficient pressure can be exerted to bring about meaningful policy change.[27]

Her work on the community of Ladakh in Northern India, or 'Little Tibet' as it is also known, is particularly striking in its demonstration of the before and after of Western 'development' and corporate globalization.[28] The Ladakh case illustrates how capitalist consumer society gradually penetrates a historically vibrant and resilient community, leaving behind a legacy of fundamental alienation and environmental pollution. We see the shift from a society built upon compassion and interdependence to one of scarcity, greed and isolation. Norberg-Hodge began visiting Ladakh in the mid-1970s. At that time, the Indian government opened this once secluded agrarian region to corporate monopolies in transportation, production and communication. Over time, the penetration of these companies and industries has ensured that local businesses cannot compete and has seriously undermined the social fabric of what Norberg-Hodge describes as 'the happiest, most vibrant people' she has ever met.

According to Norberg-Hodge, the introduction of large-scale monoculture production in Ladakh has had detrimental effects on local biodiversity through the displacement of smaller, sustainable farming methods that recognized the importance of crop diversity. She also explains how, prior to the entrance of Western corporations and the introduction of industrial production systems to the area, there was no poverty, no crime and no violence between the differing ethnic and religious communities. All of this has changed with the opening of the economy.

A community that once took pride in its own locally-produced clothing and goods is now seeking cheap Western-style consumer products. Youth in particular, seduced by Western advertising campaigns, began to seek out Western clothing, to drink Coca-Cola and to romanticize role models from Western culture with many even going so far as to use the skin lightening cream 'Fair and Lovely'. Norberg-Hodge explains the fundamental alienation linked to this process: 'Witnessing the impact of the modern world on an ancient culture gave me insights into how economic globalisation creates feelings of inadequacy and inferiority, particularly in the young, and how those psychological pressures are helping to spread the global consumer culture.'[29]

While it can be healthy and enlightening to appreciate and explore other cultures, it is quite another thing to begin to despise and reject your own culture in response. The breakdown of more collective forms of social organization deeply rooted in a cultural awareness and appreciation of interdependence has left community members, and youth in particular, feeling isolated and without hope. Drug abuse, suicide and interreligious strife, which had not previously been problems in Ladakh, have now become part of the social reality. Reflecting the harmful blend of alienation, false consciousness and exploitation discussed by socialists and socially-engaged Buddhists, the case of Ladakh highlights the ways that values get transmitted through capitalist globalization. Norberg-Hodge explains how this process is repeated across the global south:

> My experience in the South has shown me the extent to which the techno-economic structures of our society get in the way of cooperation there. I have seen people who were once cooperative become greedy and competitive under the influence of industrialization. The broader sense of self in traditional societies contrasts with the individualism of Western culture. In the West we pride ourselves on our individualism, but sometimes individualism is a euphemism for isolation. We tend to believe that a person should be completely self-sufficient, shouldn't need anybody else.[30]

And it is not just people of traditional cultures or global South countries that are being negatively impacted by capitalism. While a large proportion of the population of the global North may experience disproportionate wealth and privilege, Norberg-Hodge argues that we too are negatively affected by the messages of consumer culture:

> Over the past three decades, I have studied this process in numerous cultures around the world and discovered that we are all victims of these same psychological pressures. In virtually every industrialised country, including the US, UK, Australia, France and Japan, there is now what

is described as an epidemic of depression. In Japan, it is estimated that one million youths refuse to leave their bedrooms – sometimes for decades – in a phenomenon known as 'Hikikomori'. In the US, a growing proportion of young girls are so deeply insecure about their appearance they fall victim to anorexia and bulimia, or undergo expensive cosmetic surgery.[31]

Given that some degree of 'development' has occurred in many countries in the global South including in remote places such as Ladakh, and the profound changes resulting from industrialization and consumerism, the questions we need to ask are: What values have come with this form of development? To what degree has it served the needs of the majority? And how has it affected the environment and the capacity of future generations to meet their needs?

If the problems of Ladakh could be written off as issues of an isolated case study, we could proclaim it as the exception that proves the rule. But as the research of Norberg-Hodge and many others has made clear, centuries of capitalist 'development' and decades of 'democratization' accompanying this development, have not 'elevated' much of the Third World to the First World. As Leech states, 'The international structures under neoliberal globalization ensure that nations of the global South are perpetually "developing" and that they never actually become "developed".'[32]

We can argue that the global South's failure to become 'developed' is inevitable because bringing all countries in the world up to the level of resource consumption that exists in the First World would require four planet Earths.[33] Furthermore, such 'development' is impossible under a system that is based on exploitation and inequality, both achieved and maintained through systems of structural violence and, often, through direct physical violence such as military interventions.

This kind of structural analysis, echoing a Marxist world-view, and reflected in the perspective of the current Dalai Lama and Buddhist visionaries such as Thich Nhat Hanh, is also evident in the words of the current head of the Catholic Church, Pope Francis. In his Apostolic Exhortation of 2013, Pope Francis did not mince words when he declared, 'The thirst for power and possessions knows no limits. In this system, which tends to devour everything that stands in the way of increased profits, whatever is fragile, like the environment, is defenseless before the interests of a deified market, which becomes the only rule.'[34] He goes on to say:

Today in many places we hear a call for greater security. But until exclusion and inequality in society and between peoples are reversed, it will be impossible to eliminate violence. The poor and the poorer peoples are accused of violence, yet without equal opportunities the different forms of aggression and conflict will find a fertile terrain for growth and eventually explode. When a society – whether local, national or global – is willing to leave a part of itself on the fringes, no political programmes or resources spent on law enforcement or surveillance systems can indefinitely guarantee tranquillity. This is not the case simply because inequality provokes a violent reaction from those excluded from the system, but because the socioeconomic system is unjust at its root.[35]

Because of his 'controversial' views on capitalism and poverty, Pope Francis has been called a Marxist. US talk show host Rush Limbaugh called the Pope's Exhortation 'pure Marxism'.[36] While Stephen Moore, chief economist at the Heritage Foundation, stated, 'I think this is a Pope who clearly has some Marxist leanings. It's unquestionable that he has a very vocal scepticism (about) capitalism and free enterprise and ... I find that to be very troubling'.[37] Such assessments of the Pope's ideological leanings fail to recognize that it is his Marxist-oriented views that help him to see the global situation as clearly and compassionately as he does.

Variations on the Pope's perspective show up in many recent works that analyse the capitalist system including Leech's *Captialism: A Structural Genocide*, Naomi Klein's *This Changes Everything* and Thomas Piketty's best-selling *Capital in the Twenty-First Century*. Not even factoring in the environment – as Leech and Klein do, and which makes the structural critique all the more relevant – the arguments of renowned French economist Piketty suggest that the extreme wealth generated at one end of the system is entirely dependent upon the existence of poverty and inequality at the other end of the system. Picketty's argument closely reflects that presented by Marx 150 years earlier. In reference to capitalism's inherent tendency to generate inequality, Marx wrote, 'It makes an accumulation of misery a necessary condition, corresponding to the accumulation of wealth. Accumulation of wealth at one pole is, therefore, at the same time accumulation of misery, the torment of labour, slavery, ignorance, brutalization and moral degradation at the opposite pole'.[38]

Picketty's analysis is not new but, unlike more modest contemporary studies, he is basing his 700 pages of arguments about income and wealth inequality on a detailed analysis of data spanning 300 years and 20 different countries. What Piketty is trying to tell us with all of his numbers is that you cannot have unregulated capitalism without creating haves and have-nots. His research reveals an ever-increasing concentration of wealth and the inevitable inequality that this generates which, he argues, cannot be fixed without redistributive measures and progressive taxes on the wealthy.[39] In a similar vein, but with more radical conclusions, Leech argues that structural violence is inherent in the logic of capital because of capitalism's need to continually expand production and consumption, which is ultimately 'dependent on a process of exploitation and oppression that results in social injustice and inequality – in both power and wealth'.[40] Consequently, according to Leech, the capitalist system cannot be reformed, it must be replaced with a more democratic, humane and sustainable alternative. Meanwhile, Naomi Klein's work takes a slightly different approach, making the case that the environmental crisis caused by capitalism offers an unprecedented opportunity for activists and those who care about social justice to unite to build a global movement in which people of all political stripes can have a stake in building an alternative model.[41]

When we are able to see our lives – past, present and future – as bound up with the lives of other human beings around the world and with the planet itself (i.e. our fundamental interdependence), we can begin to see that the effects of our individual actions extend far beyond our immediate surroundings and the official political boundaries of the nation-state. Our interdependence, or interbeing, means that our wealth creation and our consumption habits have global dimensions for human beings, other animals and nature. Both Buddhism and socialism recognize this interdependence and their combined lens provides a unique view into the roots of our contemporary suffering and alienation. As Marx stated, 'Man lives from nature ... and he must maintain a continuing dialogue with it if he is not to die. To say that man's physical and mental life is linked to nature simply means that nature is linked to itself, for man is part of nature'.[42] Therefore, when we harm ourselves, we harm nature. And when we harm nature through our consumption habits, we harm ourselves. It's a simple concept that might appear obvious to a nine-year-old child, but remains beyond the comprehension of so many of us adults.

CHAPTER 5

BODIES IN THE BASEMENT

Those who do not move, do not notice their chains.
— Rosa Luxemburg

Much contemporary political activism is focused on what we need to *do* as individuals, communities and societies to confront structural violence both contemporary and historical. In an interesting parallel with what Buddhist nun Pema Chödrön advises us with regard to our individual harmful habitual patterns, Indian anti-corporate globalization activist Vandana Shiva has suggested that we could begin by doing nothing. Chödrön advises that we can begin to undo our patterns by simply and honestly recognizing them, sometimes 'on the spot', which, she says, is part of the path to wisdom even though it can feel like neurosis. Then, from that position of awareness, we may be able to stop ourselves from certain harmful or knee-jerk behaviours or responses as a stage before we are able to actually use skilful means to *do* anything. In other words, both women say that we could begin by simply recognizing the harm that we have already done (or are about to do) and by deciding to stop doing it. It soon becomes clear when we look at structural violence that this is a simple but radical suggestion. In Buddhist circles, this is part of what is called 'practice', because it is not something we always get right away and, for many of us, it is a life's work.

As I mentioned earlier, Buddhists argue that when we are attached to fixed identities – both our own or those of others – we will often go to great lengths to protect our identity, even if it means wiping out someone else's. In 2015, the Canadian Truth and Reconciliation Commission (TRC) published a harsh condemnation of the 'cultural genocide' perpetrated against indigenous peoples in Canada. In the summary of its report *Honouring the Truth: Reconciling for the Future*, the TRC states,

> For over a century, the central goals of Canada's Aboriginal policy were to eliminate Aboriginal governments; ignore Aboriginal rights; terminate the Treaties; and, through a process of assimilation, cause Aboriginal peoples to cease to exist as distinct legal, social, cultural, religious, and racial entities in Canada. The establishment and operation of residential schools were a central element of this policy, which can best be described as 'cultural genocide'.[1]

The ongoing legacy of this harm is clearly visible in the poverty, unemployment, substance abuse, alienation and the alarming rates of suicide of Canada's indigenous peoples. But often our government and sectors of the corporate media would have us deny this history in favour of one that allows us to continue living with the social structures and arrangements, or lack thereof, that continue to harm indigenous peoples.

In a 2014 article, Canadian journalist and associate editor of *Maclean's Magazine*, Tamsin McMahon, pointed out that half of First Nations children in Canada live in poverty with that figure rising to 64 per cent in the provinces of Manitoba and Saskatchewan. She notes that Aboriginal communities are likely to experience greater levels of violence, overcrowded housing and lack of access to clean drinking water. According to Statistics Canada's violent crime index, nine of Canada's ten most violent communities and 92 of Canada's 100 poorest communities are Aboriginal. The infant mortality rate in Aboriginal communities is double the national average, and First Nations children suffer disproportionately from health problems such as cavities, substance abuse, HIV-related infections and tuberculosis. As a result of this reality, Aboriginal youth 'are seven times more likely to be victims of homicide, five times more likely to commit suicide and twice as likely to die an alcohol-related death'.[2] Equally disturbing, as McMahon notes, 'The number of children taken from their homes by child welfare authorities now exceeds the number taken at the height of the residential-school era ... Aboriginal children are 10 times more likely to be placed in foster care than the Canadian average and make up half of the roughly 60,000 kids in care'.[3] So as the work of the TRC makes clear, simply recognizing a harm done – or getting others to recognize a harm done – is itself a radical political activity.

Tragically, the plight of Canada's Aboriginal peoples is not an exception. As Marxists and socialists make clear, the wealth and development of our 'advanced' capitalist societies has been predicated on genocide and slavery and continues to be dependent on the exploitation of humans, non-human animals and nature. We can thank the technological innovations and productivity of capitalism for the sheer scale of the crisis we face today, which constitutes both an environmental and an ethical problem. Our systems of production and distribution globally depend on the continuing exploitation of other peoples' land, labour and resources. Imperialism in its contemporary form continues to ensure our access to resources and, as cause and effect would have it, we then have to deal with the consequences in the form of religious fundamentalism, violence and environmental breakdown. Culturally, commodification has penetrated all spheres of life to the point that we see individuals and entire cultures either as means to our ends or as 'objects' to be removed in the interests of 'development' and 'progress'.

Historically, in the era of European colonialism, the harm done and suffering caused was justified in the name of European superiority and there was a sense of righteousness in the mission to conquer and 'civilize' distant peoples, while simultaneously engaging in outright robbery of them, their resources and their land. As Cecil Rhodes, an English capitalist who owned diamond mines in South Africa, stated in the late 1800s about the goals of colonialism, 'We must find new lands from which we can easily obtain raw materials and at the same time exploit the cheap slave labor that is available from the natives of the colonies. The colonies would also provide a dumping ground for the surplus goods produced in our factories'.[4]

It is not only the continent of Africa that is struggling to cope with the legacy of the colonial project so explicitly described by Rhodes. The gruesome realities of the genocide of indigenous peoples in the Americas and the African slave trade continue to haunt white-washed narratives of the 'discovery' of the 'New World'. And when a socialist political figure such as the Labour Party's Jeremy Corbyn suggests that schoolchildren should be taught about the negative impact and suffering caused by the British Empire, or that Britain should avoid getting caught up in endless imperialist wars in the Middle East, he is called a 'traitor' and a 'threat to national security'.[5] Like accepting the conclusions of the TRC, acknowledging the horrors of colonization or questioning the use of war as a foreign policy tool is, for some, akin to being unpatriotic.

During the colonial era, there was little pretence about equality or democracy, and certainly no discussion of human rights in the 'civilizing' mission. A country planted a flag and claimed ownership and control of an area of land. In fact, European nations saw it as their right – maybe even duty – to do so. Socialist and anti-imperialist authors such as Gerald Taiaiake Alfred, Eduardo Galeano, Samir Amin, Frantz Fanon and Edward Said have brilliantly narrated alternative views from the Americas, Africa and the Middle East to provide a more accurate telling of history.[6] All of these authors, in their own way, turn the mainstream perspective of history on its head, urging us to re-evaluate the colonial narrative while asking us to rethink the way we see the 'other' and, through this, the way we see ourselves. Speaking of his own region, Galeano explains,

> Latin America is the region of open veins. Everything from the discovery until our times, has always been transmuted in European – or later United States – capital, and as such has accumulated in distant centers of power. Everything: the soil, its fruits and its mineral-rich depth, the people and their capacity to work and to consume, natural resources and human resources. Production methods and class structure have been successively determined from outside for each area by meshing it into the universal gearbox of capitalism ... For those who see history as a competition, Latin America's backwardness and poverty are merely the result of its failure. We lost; others won. But the winners happen to have won thanks to our losing; the history of Latin America's underdevelopment is ... an integral part of the history of world capitalism's development.[7]

It is said that history is told from the perspective of the victors and nowhere is this truer than in the telling of the story of the 'Third World'. Buddhist and socialist narratives are particularly helpful in this regard in allowing us to see how the values we have internalized from our political and economic culture influence the way we see not only the present but also our past and the possibilities for the future. Viewing history as a complex web of interdependent relationships between cultures, peoples and animals and the lands they inhabit, where power and violence have systematically benefited certain groups, classes and species to the disadvantage of others, can be contrasted sharply from viewing history from the Western, linear, progress-oriented perspective. Celebrating kings and queens, generals and merchants, the rich and powerful, and basically making the realities of ordinary people often invisible is how history has generally been taught. This reality is made concrete in the names of streets, buildings and towns. In this sense, our stories and how we view ourselves reveals a lot about us. A more inclusive understanding and telling of our history is another way that we ensure we are practicing 'right view' and 'right speech'. But it is more than that. Stories of 'discovery' and 'progress' have been used, and are still being used, to justify all kinds of suffering and violence.

The Discovery Doctrine, a concept in international public law, for example, has been used to invalidate numerous indigenous land claims.[8] The Discovery Doctrine was used in North America, Australia and New Zealand by European colonizers to justify and provide a legal basis for claims over indigenous territories and control over indigenous peoples. The doctrine gave Europeans immediate rights to property seized from indigenous peoples. It was based on a belief in the superiority of the Christian European culture and the right of Europeans to exert dominance over people of other races and religions. The doctrine is still used today in legal battles over indigenous lands.[9] This doctrine is an example of how the story around an idea such as 'discovery' can become part of a system of structural violence. Even simply using the term 'discovery' is an insult to the history of indigenous peoples. As Edward Said reminds us, 'There is a difference between knowledge of other peoples and other times that is the result of understanding, compassion, careful study and analysis for their own sakes [and] that which is part of an overall campaign of self-affirmation, belligerency and outright war'.[10] This is one of many reasons why Marxists have viewed, and continue to view, the rule of law and concepts of justice under capitalism with scepticism.

Many of the alternative histories that have emerged from formerly colonized peoples have both a Marxist and a Buddhist flavour in that they are both structural (recognizing how suffering historically has been rooted in the dynamics of particular economic systems, class structures and power) and Buddhist in the sense they suggest that an empathetic orientation towards history and therefore towards other cultures (recognizing our interdependence), is critical. A more structural, compassionate and empathetic reading of history can allow us to genuinely understand both the 'other' and events from their perspective.

Having this more rigorous and compassionate orientation towards history is not just about telling our stories better – or more accurately – it has very practical advantages in terms of how we approach suffering with honesty and integrity in the here and now. In this vein, Vandana Shiva convincingly argues that without a correct understanding of history we cannot properly address contemporary problems such as poverty. She points out that the reading of history presented by mainstream economists such as Jeffrey Sachs suggests that in the great process of wealth generation resulting from the Industrial Revolution, 'much of the world was left far behind'.[11] This, she suggests, is a complete misreading of history:

> The poor are not those who have been 'left behind'; they are the ones who have been robbed. The riches accumulated by Europe are based on riches taken from Asia, Africa and Latin America. Without the destruction of India's rich textile industry, without the takeover of the spice trade, without the genocide of the native American tribes, without Africa's slavery, the Industrial Revolution would not have led to new riches for Europe or the US. It was this violent takeover of Third World resources and markets that created wealth in the North and poverty in the South.[12]

In this sense, it becomes important not only to have the 'right view' about current issues but to acknowledge that our interdependence extends far back into our pasts. This allows us to see that current wealth and privilege has been built on historical structural violence. The purpose of this is not to make those of us born in wealthy countries feel guilty – although some of us will inevitably feel this way. I didn't personally cause the genocide of the indigenous in North America, but I have to take responsibility for the fact that my society did and that my personal privilege today is a consequence of that genocide. That is what the painstaking and dedicated work of the Canadian TRC has been about. But it becomes clear that taking a hard, systematic and honest look at the history of our capitalist economic system allows us to gain a more grounded perspective on how we got to be where we are and how we may proceed so as not to continue causing the kind of suffering that many analysts from global South and indigenous communities speak about. Once we have an understanding of our alienation in contemporary society, we can begin to understand the roots of our suffering both as individuals and as broader cultures.

So what are some of the concrete ways that alienation manifests in our economy and society, and how may we begin to confront these realities? One day when I was thinking about this issue, I wondered what it would be like if we knew immediately the consequences of our actions. Buddhists talk about karma and scientists about cause and effect, but essentially both are addressing the idea that every action produces some kind of reaction. In the case of karma, it's not about being punished for transgressions or 'getting what we deserve', as popular thinking would have it, but rather simply recognizing that our actions, whether we think of them as positive or negative, have consequences, often far beyond what we imagine.[13]

Pondering this reality led me to imagine the concept of a warning system that I rather gruesomely labelled as the 'bodies in the basement' approach. For example, we would immediately at point-of-purchase see the entanglement of our cell phone purchase with the fate of children engaged in coltan mining in the Congo who are facing violence, the rape of their mothers, and not being able to attend school; or as we stood in line to order a Big Mac we would reflect on the fact that due to our heavily meat-based diet we are dependent upon a system of raising livestock that is the single largest contributor of greenhouse gas emissions globally; or we would witness the working conditions of the Bangladeshi sweatshop worker as we were about to purchase a new shirt; or as we turned our heating system on we had a vision of the skin problems and respiratory diseases afflicting communities living on or near land owned by multinational coal mining companies; or as we pulled out our credit card to buy new cotton pants we realized that over 200,000 unsubsidized Indian farmers had committed suicide because they couldn't compete with the heavily-subsidized cotton growers in wealthy nations; or looking at the menu in a restaurant we would witness the mental health problems of slaughterhouse workers, and so on.

I envisioned that people, after seriously reflecting on these gruesome realities that are currently hidden from them (i.e. bodies in the basement), would have to choose which of two buttons they had to push before making their purchase. The first button would declare, 'Yes, I know what this means but I'm still going to do it'. The second button would state, 'No, I guess I don't really need to buy or eat this thing or do this activity'. In other words, it would require people to act mindfully, to understand the consequences of their choices.

Without getting bogged down about the practicalities – or impracticalities – of such an approach to addressing structural violence, imagine how it would impact the world if we did this in some form or another as individuals, as parents, as workers, as communities, as countries? Now you may think, isn't this all a bit preachy and guilt-inducing, and wouldn't such a process likely lead us to lock ourselves in our homes and do or buy nothing? I don't think so. Not if we believe that alternative social and economic arrangements are possible.

But socialists would remind us that individual solutions like shopping ethically or recycling or cycling to work, while they are all important and help us to shift our perspectives and to encourage new ways of living, they are not enough because our problems are rooted in the broader structures and institutional arrangements of the capitalist system. It is true that we cannot individually stop global warming and human exploitation by solely engaging in an alternative lifestyle or by simply shopping ethically and even if we hoped we could over the long haul, environmental scientists of all political persuasions tell us we just don't have that kind of time. Just as the problems extend from the individual to the societal level, so do the solutions. For instance, many of the changes we would need to make can be difficult at an individual level, such as finding an alternative to using the petrol at our local gas station when we live in an area with no or inadequate public transportation. It is also difficult to transform our eating habits in order to confront the ethical and environmental implications of factory farming when we can only afford heavily-subsidized processed foods instead of expensive, unsubsidized natural and organic alternatives.

So, while our individual choices have meaning and do contribute to shifts in behaviours and values, ultimately we have to confront our economic system. Socialist David Nibert argues that while getting rid of capitalism will not mean that people will instantly behave more ethically with regard to their treatment of humans and non-human animals, its demise is a necessary precondition for such a shift in behaviour. He identifies three reasons for this: elite control of public consciousness, elite control of the state, and 'the economic marginalization and financial struggles that consume the mass of the citizenry'.[14] In other words, if people are just trying to get by and to survive (the reality of most of humanity under global capitalism), there is not much likelihood that they will focus on the broader ethical concerns necessary to lead us to a socially just world. Ultimately, the very structures of corporate capitalism must be confronted in order to make it possible to end the structural violence that our lifestyles in the global North are dependent upon.

Making the bodies in the basement visible is a task that could be grounded in a socialist view highlighting the links between our capitalist institutions and processes, the values and lifestyles that depend upon them, the corresponding misery and violence faced by much of our planet's population and the harm done to non-human animals and nature. From a socialist perspective the bodies in the basement can be directly tied to the prioritization of capital accumulation over human wellbeing in the capitalist economy. Combining this approach with a Buddhist view would help us to see how these connections are a product of our interdependence and would provide us with the opportunity to take collective responsibility for our choices in a compassionate way. The alternative is to continue with what we currently have: a system in which we engage mindlessly in many activities that negatively affect humans, other animals and nature on a daily basis with the consequences remaining largely invisible to us. And as many have been saying for decades, we may end up without a planet upon which to make even bad choices if we don't change our tack. But the idealist in me believes that if the lines of interdependence were made more visible, many of us would make more compassionate choices and, for those who didn't, at least there would be a conscious recognition that a choice is being made. If we knowingly make poor choices then not only will we feel uncomfortable and guilty (even if only subconsciously), but we will also entrench ourselves in our alienated condition and remain disconnected from ourselves and others.

As I mentioned earlier, for many of us in the global North, the consequences of our actions are not visible and we are not urged to seek them out. In fact we are constantly distracted from them by corporate media and advertising. I really don't believe it is because we are bad people or that we somehow want to hurt others or destroy the planet. But we have a problem that is connected to what Buddhist eco-philosopher Joanna Macy and physician Chris Johnstone call the 'business as usual' view. They note,

When you're in the middle of this story, it's easy to think of it as just the way things are. Young people may be told there is no alternative but to find their place in this scheme of things. Getting ahead is presented as the main plot, supported by the subplots of finding a partner, fending for your family, looking good, and buying stuff. In this view of life, the problems of the world are seen as far away and irrelevant to the dramas or our personal lives.[15]

If the current corporate capitalist model is seen as perfectly rational and indeed desirable by those benefiting from it – which includes many of us in the global North – then why would those benefactors in positions of power and influence promote or even allow change? Why would companies that make billions of dollars from our mindless consumption want us to make 'right view' choices that would negatively impact their bottom line? What incentives are there to make those choices ourselves or to ask others to make them? We have to go out of our way to *see* the structural violence resulting from our actions and even further out of our way to *do* something about it.

So how does acknowledging the 'bodies in the basement' help us? And how does our access to information about the bodies get blocked? Italian socialist Antonio Gramsci's theory of hegemony explains how the capitalist system contains various mechanisms to gain our consent (i.e. socialization through education and media) or tools of coercion (i.e. laws, police, courts and prisons) to ensure our subservience.[16] Corporations have not hesitated to use such coercive tactics to ensure that no light is shed on the bodies in the basement. For instance, Oprah Winfrey was sued for millions of dollars for suggesting that hamburgers may not be the best thing for our health.[17] Similarly, British environmental activists Helen Steel and David Morris spent over 20 years of their lives and thousands of pounds in a battle with McDonald's. The now infamous McLibel case in the 1990s was the longest trial in English history, in which the fast food giant sued community gardener Steel and postman Morris over a little pamphlet they and others from London Greenpeace (not to be confused with Greenpeace International which the couple refused to join) wrote criticizing McDonald's for its labour, human and animal rights and environmental impacts.[18]

Examples such as these abound and are illustrative of the lengths to which corporations will go to avoid responsibility and to protect their brand name. And new cases are arising all over the world. As previously mentioned, corporations go to great lengths to ensure that the barbaric practices used on factory farms where our food animals are raised are entirely hidden from us. In discussions surrounding the US-EU Transatlantic Trade and Investment Partnership (TTIP), US food companies have vigorously argued against labelling food as 'genetically modified', claiming it is a restriction on free trade.[19] Meanwhile, sugar companies have pressured the World Health Organization to change its guidelines on healthy eating, deeming them to have been too strict with regard to the amount of sugar people should be consuming.[20] The sugar industry has also worked with US government researchers to soften federal recommendations on sugar intake.[21] And some corporations have been accused of resorting to direct physical violence by intimidating and killing community members and union leaders, particularly in global South countries. In Colombia alone, Drummond Mining, Coca-Cola and Occidental Petroleum have faced such accusations. And Chiquita Brands pled guilty in US Federal Court in 2007 to providing $1.7 million in funding to a Colombian right-wing paramilitary group on the US State Department's terrorist list.[22] It is clear that those who dominate our economic system will go to great lengths and expense to defend their profits and, through their ownership of the media, control what we see and hear. As noted earlier, this is not a conspiracy, it is simply a rational component of a corporate controlled economic system that prioritizes the accumulation of capital.

But as we start to count the bodies in the basement, we begin to realize the degree to which we are interconnected with our fellow global citizens through the global capitalist economy. For instance, let's take a brief look at something as benign-sounding as coltan, a dull black metallic ore. It is inside *every* smart phone. There is no obvious substitute. We also use it in other consumer electronics, and it is considered a 'strategic mineral' by military experts. About a quarter of the world's coltan production comes from conflict zones in Central Africa while an illegal coltan industry controlled by paramilitaries and Mexican drug cartels is emerging across the borders of Colombia, Venezuela and Brazil in South America. In her article 'Two Children May Have Died For You to Have Your Mobile Phone', Inés Benitez of the Tierramérica Network addresses the conflict in the Democratic Republic of the Congo, where over 60 per cent of the world's coltan supplies are located. As she explains, 'The extraction of coltan contributes to maintaining one of the bloodiest armed conflicts in Africa, which has led to more than five million deaths, massive displacements of the population, and the rape of 300,000 women in the last 15 years, according to human rights organisations'.[23] Endangered elephants and gorillas are also threatened by coltan mining in the region's national parks.

Meanwhile, in China, the company that produces the Samsung, Sony and Dell smartphones that use coltan, as well as those cool Apple gadgets that we like so much, has been the site of numerous worker suicides. Foxconn's Longhua facility, which has over 400,000 employees making close to 140,000 iPhones a day – that's 90 every minute – faced international criticism when it was revealed that workers were throwing themselves out of office windows. A disturbing aspect of this case was the company's response. While the company has paid reparations to families of the deceased, the most striking and perhaps revealing response they had was to construct nets around the building. I always have to take a brief pause after telling my students this, because this strategy to address the symptom rather than the cause of the problem literally leaves me speechless. And then, after six suicides in 2010, Foxconn asked a group of Buddhist monks to bless the company during this 'difficult' time and proceeded to organize 'venting rooms' that contained punching bags with the faces of Foxconn executives on them.[24]

While some in the global North may dismiss this case as part of the broader human rights problem in China or a bizarre expression of some foreign culture, it may behoove us to explore the degree to which all capitalist societies have been busy stringing metaphorical nets (such as drugs for depression and anxiety) and creating virtual punching bags (reality shows or Hollywood movies that contain a critique of capitalism like the *Wolf of Wall Street* or for kids *Wall-E* and *The Lego Movie*) in an attempt to avoid seriously confronting the causes of the outcomes and neuroses generated by an unjust, alienating and unsustainable economic system.

The sorts of human rights issues related to capitalist production that exist in China can be found throughout the global South. A few years ago I worked with a Canadian grassroots group, the Atlantic Regional Solidarity Network, on a campaign to bring awareness to human rights violations in Colombia connected to the use of electricity in my home community in Canada.[25] The power companies of both my home province of Nova Scotia and the neighbouring province of New Brunswick were purchasing coal from the Cerrejón Mine in Colombia – the largest open pit coal mine in the world stretching 45 kilometres in length and 8 kilometres in width and owned by three of the world's largest multinational mining companies. In addition to causing massive environmental degradation, the mine's owners were engaged in displacing Afro-Colombian and indigenous Wayuu communities to facilitate the constant expansion of the mine.

The idea of the campaign was to show how every time we switched on our lights that someone in Colombia would suffer. I think it's safe to say that a majority of Atlantic Canadians had – and despite our campaign probably still have – no idea where the coal that generates their electricity comes from. And why would they? Most people we spoke to were shocked to hear the stories of the communities displaced or in threat of displacement and to see how communities still living near the mine were facing serious mental and physical health problems associated with mining activity. The plight of the Colombian villagers constituted a clear case of structural violence made invisible by complex chains of production and consumption and a good dose of corporate public relations.

In the broader picture, mining activity in Latin America, as socialist historian Eduardo Galeano so poetically makes clear in his classic book *The Open Veins of Latin America*, has always involved massive human rights violations and environmental destruction. It would be nice if we could say that this sector is exceptional in some way, but viewed from a socialist or socially-engaged Buddhist perspective, we can see that in almost every industry under corporate globalization, from mining to energy to manufacturing to agriculture, we can find these largely invisible links of interdependence and bodies in the basement. Structural violence is expressed in many forms, some are closer to home than we realize. What we consume every day of our lives, in other words the sources of our electricity, our clothes, our gasoline and even our food, are inescapably linked to the lives of other human beings, non-human animals and the environment.

There is perhaps no more personal and intimate an example of our interconnectedness than the essential relationship we have with nature and those who grow the food that we eat in order to remain alive. Buddhists have long pointed to this fact as something to celebrate but also as a reason to be particularly mindful of what we are putting in our mouths. Marxists are also well aware of the political significance of food and food systems, historically spending a great deal of time exploring the development of capitalist agriculture and the inevitable exploitation of labour, land and animals associated with it. As a person who loves to cook and eat, I have spent many hours thinking about food and how what I choose to eat is a personal, conscious daily activity linking me with other beings and the problem of structural violence. It is one area in our economic system that I (and many others) have discovered to be particularly convoluted.

I recently returned from spending three months living with my family in a downtown neighbourhood in Havana, Cuba. I would venture out each day to the cooperative farmers' markets just blocks from our apartment to purchase fresh, locally-grown, organic vegetables. Right across the street from our Havana apartment, a woman was selling fresh natural juices: tamarind, mango and guayaba. I couldn't help but reflect on the high cost of natural (not 'fresh' exactly) juices at our local Canadian grocery store compared with say Coca-Cola or Sprite.

Very quickly, we found ourselves buying nearly all of our food in our Havana neighbourhood while chatting and getting to know the folks up and down our street. Within a short time, our young boys were heading out by themselves to the neighbourhood baker a couple of blocks away to buy fresh bread in the mornings. The 'bread lady', as my kids affectionately referred to her, was thrilled to see the boys and would often give them an extra roll. An old man who sold homemade jam would stop them each morning and share stories in his broken English. We walked everywhere and, with very little effort, my partner lost 25 pounds and we all felt very healthy. We had to go out of our way to get to a shopping mall that sold processed goods which were, relatively speaking, quite expensive. And there were no McDonalds or Kentucky Fried Chicken outlets to tempt me on my way home from work. In short, it was inconvenient and expensive to eat unhealthily in Havana, which is the exact opposite of North America.

It is not a coincidence that socialist Cuba is the *only* country in the world to have achieved sustainable development. In other words, Cuba is meeting the basic needs – food, housing, healthcare and education – of its entire population in an ecologically sustainable manner. Certainly, Cubans are not living extravagant lives, and there are issues with low salaries and a housing shortage. But homelessness, malnutrition, illiteracy and violent crime are conspicuous by their absence in Cuba. Furthermore, the country has an average life expectancy as well as infant and child mortality rates that compare to First World nations.[26]

Many Cubans laughed when I talked excitedly about their fruit and vegetable markets. While they eat a lot of them, fresh organic vegetables are considered by most Cubans to be 'poor people's food'. In the shopping mall, well-dressed Cubans eat fried chicken, French fries and hamburgers while drinking soda pop. Many Cubans aspire to having more meat and processed food in their diet, associating these products with being more 'developed'. And they are not alone in the global South in this desire. As researchers such as Helena Norberg-Hodge have shown in their cross-cultural studies, exposure to Western media and advertising and the penetration of Western corporate chains has led a great deal of the world's population to aspire to a Western lifestyle including its unhealthy and unsustainable aspects.[27] We can see that to some degree the idea that the capitalist consumer culture and things like fast food are signs of 'development' has penetrated even in a socialist country such as Cuba where alternative values are expressed institutionally. Much of this influence has come through tourism, one area of the Cuban economy actively engaging with the capitalist world.

At the root of this is an insidious structural violence that plays out differently in the global North and global South. In the South the ability to be a consumer and in particular to consume particular products identified in Western movies and advertising becomes a sign of being advanced and successful. In the global North, these same pressures exist but the domination in our grocery stores of cheap, unhealthy, usually genetically-modified, corporate-manufactured foods loaded with sodium and sugar has led to massive increases in heart disease, diabetes and obesity.[28] Corporate subsidies have allowed for the mass production of cheap processed foods while locally-produced, environmentally-friendly, non-GM food is too expensive for many families. In this context, we should not be surprised by the 'choices' people make or by the constantly rising costs of healthcare. Processed foods are artificially inexpensive due to the massive taxpayer subsidies that agri-businesses receive. If those subsidies were shifted over to locally-based organic food producers then the cost difference between junk food and healthy food would diminish significantly.

Sure, a person might still choose McDonalds even if there was an equally delicious and affordable organic vegetable dish offered as an alternative to a Big Mac, but at least they would think about the fact that they are making a choice (with all the caveats about how limited this 'choice' may be, given the power of advertising and years of developing particular tastes). In our contemporary food systems, we have little power to influence or even to fully understand and see how our choices – and food prices – are determined long before we order the chicken nuggets. Marxists would identify capitalist control of the food production and distribution system as the reason for this. From a socialist perspective, this system is completely authoritarian and, with the accumulation of capital as its central goal, it is incapable of meeting either the nutritional or the broader health needs of a growing global population. And, at the end of the day, we need to ask ourselves if options that are statistically proven to harm our health and to be destructive to non-human animals and nature should be the most readily available choices. From a Buddhist perspective, we would have to ask how our interdependence with all beings implies a responsibility to ensure that our most basic need to feed ourselves is met by our food production systems and that these systems do the least amount of harm possible to humans, non-human animals and nature.

But the profit-making in junk food goes beyond the food producers. When we become sick and overweight and depressed because of all the nutritionally poor, high sugar, high fat food that we eat, in conjunction with our increasingly sedentary lifestyles, pharmaceutical companies eagerly offer their products to 'help' us feel better.[29] And in our current healthcare approach in North America, we are socialized to think about treatment rather than prevention. This is reflected in everything from drug plans (how many of us can get coverage to see a naturopath or get a massage?) to medical school curricula (where are the nutrition classes?). We increasingly pay lip service to prevention in schools and workplaces, but the structural reality reduces our preventative healthcare options to relying on either our family's resources (and social capital reflected in education, gym memberships, time to work out, etc.) or our personal willpower to keep healthy in the face of constant temptation.

At the same time, the structural violence resulting from our dietary habits is proving devastating not only for us but for non-human animals and the planet itself. Drawing on research from the Worldwatch Institute, the US Environmental Protection Agency and various academics, the documentary film *Cowspiracy: The Sustainability Secret* points to animal agriculture as 'the leading cause of species extinction, ocean dead zones, water pollution, and habitat destruction'.[30] The Food and Agriculture Organization (FAO) of the United Nations has argued that livestock production alone is the single largest contributor to greenhouse gas emissions, producing 18 per cent of the global total and surpassing all forms of transportation combined.

But researchers at the World Bank disagreed with the methodology used by the FAO, which did not include livestock respiration in its calculations. In their 2009 report, Robert Goodland, former lead environmental adviser at the World Bank, and Jeff Anhang, senior research officer at the Bank's International Finance Corporation, made their stunning conclusion that livestock and their by-products actually account for up to 32,000 million tons of CO_2 per year, or 51 per cent of all worldwide greenhouse gas emissions. According to Goodland and Anhang, 'Although methane warms the atmosphere much more strongly than does CO_2 its half-life in the atmosphere is only about 8 years versus at least 100 years for CO_2. As a result, a significant reduction in livestock raised worldwide would reduce GHGs relatively quickly compared with measures involving renewable energy and energy efficiency'.[31] Last time I checked, the World Bank was not a raging green activist organization. Remember, they're the folks that, along with the IMF and the WTO, brought us corporate globalization and its corresponding austerity agenda. The fact that they're making these arguments should really wake us up to how extreme this particular problem is.

The FAO also states that the livestock sector is by far the largest single user of land globally with 26 per cent of the Earth's ice-free land used for grazing. Meanwhile, the grain we feed livestock animals requires approximately one-third of all arable land and is a central contributor to deforestation.[32] Cattle ranching in the Brazilian Amazon – driven by the international beef and leather trades – accounts for approximately 80 per cent of all deforestation in the region and, according to Greenpeace, about 14 per cent of the world's total annual deforestation. The FAO reports that 70 per cent of the deforestation that had occurred in the Amazon by 1995, and over 90 per cent of deforestation since, is due to cattle ranching.[33] To top it all off nicely, the livestock sector is responsible for 65 per cent of 'anthropogenic nitrous oxide' emissions, mostly from cow shit. The US Environmental Protection Agency says that 'Nitrous oxide molecules stay in the atmosphere for an average of 114 years before being removed by a sink or destroyed through chemical reactions. The impact of 1 pound of N2O on warming the atmosphere is almost 300 times that of 1 pound of carbon dioxide'.[34]

As socialists would remind us, the solution to a structural problem of such massive proportions must also be structural. It is unrealistic to expect to be able to get cheap, locally-produced tropical mango juice or bananas where I live on Cape Breton Island in Nova Scotia. However, it is not unrealistic to think about subsidized cooperative food systems that provide locally-produced fruits and vegetables and to complement them with regional markets that allow us to fulfil most of our remaining dietary needs. It is also not unrealistic to think about re-educating ourselves in order to reconnect with the cycles of nature and the seasonal availability of certain produce and to think about how we take into consideration communities that don't have access to fertile land and so on.

Talking about food lets us see how privilege and empowerment works in capitalist society. I am part of a privileged sector of society so I can choose to eat organic, and where possible, locally-produced foods, and can at an individual level feel somewhat empowered doing so because I am making good choices for my personal health and the health of my family. I can also choose not to shop at Walmart or eat at Burger King and feel good about that too. I can afford to pay out of pocket to visit a naturopath once or twice a year. But the socialist in me realizes that when I want my society to consider prioritizing making healthy food a more obvious and accessible choice for my fellow citizens and to stop the suffering related to consumer goods – cheap labour, human and non-human animal rights abuses, and unsustainable environmental practices – I am completely disempowered. My personal privilege allows me to make a lot of individual choices that make me feel better in my individual life, but like many in my culture, I am increasingly alienated by the values that dominate capitalist society and I can't feel entirely good about my choices when others are not able to make these same choices. As Woody Allen's character Alvy Singer says in the film *Annie Hall*, 'If one guy is starving someplace, that puts a crimp in my evening', and socially engaged Buddhists would say, 'and so it should!'.

This alienation and related disempowerment goes to the heart of why individual awareness is critical but, at the same time, collective and structural responses and changes are necessary. As noted by Jonathan Safran Foer,

> It shouldn't be the consumer's responsibility to figure out what's cruel and what's kind, what's environmentally destructive and what's sustainable. Cruel and destructive food products should be illegal. We don't need the option of buying children's toys made with lead paint, or aerosols with chlorofluorocarbons, or medicines with unlabelled side effects. And we don't need the option of buying factory farmed animals.[35]

We also don't need to purchase heavily-subsidized US cotton that is contributing to the deaths of India's small farmers, or coltan that is trapping Africans in violence and poverty, or computer gadgets that are immiserating Chinese workers, or food that contributes to cruelty, labour rights violations and massive environmental and health problems.

So, as Marx correctly noted, we all make history, but not in circumstances of our own choosing. And, to echo Schumacher, the problem of production has not been solved. As long as we see ourselves as separate from each other and as long as we try to solve these problems through individual activities, whether drugs, alcohol or hot yoga, the economic system that enforces our separateness literally feeds upon and reinforces this isolation and alienation because it makes economic sense to do so. And as long as we feel incomplete, we will constantly seek out experiences and products to fill the void. Misery makes an amazing market.

As we have seen, all of these harms are rooted in systems of production and distribution which we as individuals contribute to but as individuals acting alone cannot change. For this reason we must become aware of the bodies in the basement that result from our individual choices and work collectively for systemic change. But we must first understand the true nature of the beast that lies at the core of our alienation and related suffering.

CHAPTER 6

CAPITALISM AND THE DEMOCRATIC DEFICIT

Democracy no longer means what it was meant to.
It has been taken back into the workshop. Each of its
institutions has been hollowed out, and it has been
returned to us as a vehicle for the free market, of the
corporations. For the corporations, by the corporations.

— Arundhati Roy

All of the arguments I have made so far in this book speak to a rethinking of how we share this planet. I have tried to show how overcoming alienation involves what Buddhists identify as a recognition of our fundamental interdependence with other human beings, non-human animals and nature. We have looked at how socially-engaged Buddhists and socialists highlight the nature of our contemporary forms of alienation, how these get expressed in individual and structural violence and how interdependence is demonstrated in our daily activities of work and consumption. Given this global reality, what becomes clear is that our commonly accepted ideas about nationally-based citizenship and democracy, where compassion to our fellow human beings and other animals is conditional and limited by state boundaries, are clearly not tenable in a globalized, interdependent world. In a way, we have outgrown them. Marxists would argue that our Western liberal views of democracy were never tenable because they have always existed alongside an authoritarian and exploitative economic system. Socially-engaged Buddhists would argue that all boundaries, borders and walls that are maintained through coercion and violence are ultimately just reflections of our delusion of separateness – the idea that we must protect ourselves against the 'other'. This is not to suggest that we have no cultural differences or uniqueness, but rather to highlight that living as beings on an interdependent planet necessitates a new kind of global citizenship rooted in the idea of what the Dalai Lama calls the 'single family' of humanity. As he explains, 'We need to embrace the oneness of humanity and show concern for everyone – not just my family or my country or my continent. We must show concern for every being not just the few who resemble us. Differences of religion, ideology, race, economic system, social system, and government are all secondary'.[1]

As I have argued throughout this book, climate change, ecological degradation and the finite nature of the fossil fuels upon which our lifestyles depend bring a certain urgency to recognizing our interdependence and demand that we re-evaluate the boundaries and practices of contemporary democracy. As a socialist perspective makes clear, the ongoing exploitation of nature and of humans and other animals upon which the current economic system of capitalism depends is not only ethically problematic, it may ultimately undermine the future of life on this planet.

Belief systems and organizational arrangements of citizenship and accountability are intimately linked. But, as a socially engaged Buddhist perspective helps to make clear, under capitalism where our delusion of separateness is reinforced, they are delinked to the degree that suffering on one end of the system – where communities are displaced or face human rights violations due to 'development' projects, or where biodiversity is devastated, or where animals face systematic abuse – is not acknowledged or compensated on the other end of the system where a minority benefits economically through profits and through access to particular resources and goods such as cheap oil, genetically-modified foods and other consumer products.

There are two arguments commonly used to justify the current forms and practices of contemporary democracy and citizenship. First, due to the high level of rights and living standards in the global North, many argue that, while flawed, our liberal democratic system is basically working; and second, global or universal visions of citizenship cannot work because human communities are bounded by cultural, ethnic and national identities – we're all too different and we live in different places.

As discussed in previous chapters, the ideology of individualism reinforces our sense of separateness and our feeling that our failure to succeed or to get what we need from the system is our own fault. In addition, citizenship under capitalism has been focused on individuals as holders of rights within the bounded territory of the nation-state. This view has been reinforced and protected by our Western legal traditions. Notwithstanding specific laws to deal with issues such as multiculturalism and language protection, the Western tradition prioritizes individual rights over collective rights. Ideas about democratic citizenship have emphasized an active individual 'agent' (i.e. a person of legal age with voting rights who is protected by the various rights enshrined in a constitution). According to theory, this person actively participates in political processes that ensure transparency and accountability. Because of this, we may accept certain assumptions of the commonly-held view of citizenship; for example, that people live in bounded communities and have certain values, ways of being and traditions that they seek to nurture and protect. And, furthermore, it makes sense that people living in particular territorial boundaries should have a disproportionate say in what happens within those boundaries.

But, as we saw in the previous chapters, liberal democracies in 'advanced' capitalist countries, while delivering high standards of living and rights for many, still fall far short in delivering on accountability and equality within their own borders let alone in their international relations. The dire situation of indigenous peoples both in Canada and the United States and the ongoing disproportionate levels of poverty of other racialized groups in these countries make this painfully evident. The Institute for Research on Poverty in the United States shows that according to the 2013 Census Report, 46.5

million people, or 15 per cent of the total US population, were living in poverty. According to the report, 'Blacks and Hispanics have poverty rates that greatly exceed the average'.[2] Meanwhile, the Canadian Government Census reports 1.1 million racialized persons living in poverty in Canada in 2006. While constituting only 4 per cent of the total population, racialized persons accounted for 32 per cent of all persons living in poverty.

When we look at the global level we realize that we are not even in the ballpark of attaining democratic accountability and equality. Global North countries, through their elected leaders and economic elites, have a disproportionately large influence over the mechanics of our global capitalist system. But it is only the citizens of the wealthy countries who vote for the political leaders in those powerful nations; political leaders that wield a hugely disproportionate amount of influence in global politics. And with regard to some of the world's most powerful decision-makers – corporate CEOs and the heads of the IMF and the World Bank – they are not democratically elected by any of us. How can that be? How can it be that we passively accept that our democratic systems do not hold many of the most influential decision-makers to account? Socialists would strongly argue that liberal democracies will never be able to properly address this problem because of the limited scope of accountability in the economic realm in capitalist societies. The process of globalization has further intensified this problem in increasingly insidious ways as countries around the world have simultaneously experienced 'democratization' in Western liberal terms alongside ongoing imperialism, structural violence and various degrees of impotence in international decision-making bodies.

I am going to make a couple of assumptions here. I like to think that most citizens in the global North would probably agree that democracy is not just about rights but also includes responsibilities, and that a fundamental underpinning of a genuine democracy is accountability. I believe these to be fairly safe assumptions, particularly in societies where the Protestant work ethic is pervasive and there is at least a pretence towards the idea that we shouldn't receive benefits that we haven't earned nor do we take away benefits that rightfully belong to others. But what do these values have to do with our current decision-making processes under corporate globalization?

We have seen how under conditions of economic globalization, the rallying cry is 'free trade' and 'open borders', and implicit in this is the rather romantic narrative of the 'global village'. Walking through many major North American airports, for example, one can see the vivid and beautiful images, multicultural global scenes and clever turns of phrase that accompany the HSBC bank's advertising campaigns. As Andrea Newman, HSBC's group head of advertising states, 'We're very much focused on the sort of person who has an international outlook. That's not necessarily someone jumping on and off planes, but someone who is interested in the world. Maybe they work for a global company and need to travel for work.'[3]

The global images presented by HSBC are accompanied by words like love, responsibility, winner, loser, accomplishment and privilege, along with phrases such as 'Never underestimate the importance of local knowledge', 'Be part of the future, your DNA will be your data' and 'The food chain and the supply chain will merge'. There is also the image of three traditionally-attired African girls with the statement, '0.3% of Saharan solar energy could power Europe. Do you see potential? We do'. Even the most radical Marxist, while staving off nausea, has to be impressed with this campaign. The idea of the global village clearly excites people and, hopefully, from the corporate perspective, excites consumers and investors. Who could disagree with open borders and more trade among nations? Surely this is the way to increase peace and prosperity for us all. Isn't this what global interdependence is all about?

As former World Bank economist Joseph Stiglitz has pointed out, while talk of trade agreements may cause the eyes of most of us to glaze over, we should be paying attention if we care about genuine democracy. Hiding in the neutral-sounding language of international trade agreements are a bunch of authoritarian policies that threaten democratic accountability everywhere they are implemented. Despite the fact that he is a world-renowned economist who has been part of the international economic establishment responsible for creating, managing and maintaining the current global economic order, Stiglitz suggests that ignoring this reality could put us on 'the wrong side of globalization' because trade agreements such as the Trans-Pacific Partnership (TPP) contain 'a real risk that it will benefit the wealthiest sliver of the American and global elite at the expense of everyone else'.[4]

The TPP is a free trade agreement between twelve Pacific Rim countries reached on 5 October 2015 that creates the largest free trade area in the world. Mostly negotiated in secrecy, as is common with these agreements, it is seen by the United States as a partnership agreement to the TTIP agreement reached with Europe mentioned earlier. Leaked drafts of the TTIP have caused some controversy. Like the agreement with Europe, the TPP contains measures to lower trade barriers such as tariffs and establish a dispute resolution process. In reality, Stiglitz points out, tariff barriers are already low, unlike when these types of agreements were signed after World War Two. Pushed by the corporate sector, the focus in this agreement is on 'non-tariff barriers' such as regulations which, when one looks beyond the jargon, are mechanisms that countries establish to protect workers, consumers and the environment. According to Stiglitz, 'The fact that such a plan is under consideration at all is testament to how deeply inequality reverberates through our economic policies'.[5] While the pretence is to establish 'regulatory harmony', the goal is to remove mechanisms that, for the most part, were established 'by governments responding to the democratic demands of their citizens'.[6] From a Marxist perspective, free trade and regulatory harmony are simply the most recent expressions of capitalism's requirement for the 'continuous expansion of the spheres of both production and circulation' as the maximization of profits are prioritized over everything else.[7] And from a socially-engaged Buddhist perspective, the TPP highlights how we need to examine all the spaces where equality and accountability are undermined, because likely harm is being done. The harm may find expression in lack of access to housing, healthcare, schooling or food. In addition, Buddhists would emphasize the welfare of others as a primary consideration of all of our actions and policies.

But the ideology propelling the system, reinforced by our media and education systems, tells a different story. The first thing that becomes obvious when we begin to unpack this model is the glaring bias in the arguments and practices of most proponents of economic globalization. While making the pretence that economic opening is about how we can all share our cultures, ways of life and ingenuity, and that trading with other nations and getting their investment are inherently good things, the reality is that there are only certain people who can actually take advantage of the kind of opening that capitalist globalization entails. In reality, and indeed often in law, the focus of this 'opening' is the interests of economic actors, and the 'rights' are for the largest and most powerful of these actors.

We return to bodies in the basement. The sheer misery of many and the poverty and inequality faced by a majority of the people in the global south – and increasing numbers in the global North – under capitalism is a wake-up call for those of us who benefit disproportionately from this system. Even if we could say that it's all the fault of the peoples of the global South – their cultures, their governments, their religions, their race – which is clearly not the case, Buddhists would say that all of this is irrelevant at the end of the day if we view humanity from the perspective of interdependence and that constantly upholding the welfare of others is a key value. An analysis of North–South relations suggests that there is an ongoing structural and institutional bias in the global system favouring the cultures and economies of the global North whether we examine decisions of the United Nations Security Council or the policies of our major global economic institutions.

The economic opening process in the global South has largely been facilitated by the IMF, whose programmes of economic reform, also known as Structural Adjustment Programs (SAPs), are reinforced by the WTO and have been part of the global South reality for over 30 years. As noted earlier, despite more than three decades of economic globalization, so-called development still eludes most of humanity. The focus in these programs is 'macroeconomic stabilization', efficiency and growth. These involve a blend of policies that always includes some mix of fiscal austerity to balance budgets, the privatization of state-run enterprises and a reduction in barriers to foreign investment, in other words, deregulation. And therein lies the rub. There is no objective angle to argue for deregulation. It, like all policies promoted by the IMF, the World Bank and the WTO, has very real ideological implications. For instance, many of the regulatory frameworks established by national governments following World War Two have been a way to protect ourselves from harm or suffering caused by economic activity: harm to workers, harm to consumers, harm to the environment and, at a more systemic level, harm to our democratic rights. We could say that within the flawed capitalist system, regulations are one way that populations have attempted to ensure the protection of the welfare of majorities.

Healthcare and education services are examples of how these harms manifest themselves. Many of us believe that access to basic healthcare and education should be fundamental rights of citizens in democratic societies and for socially-engaged Buddhists and socialists this goes without saying. Indeed, the United Nations Convention on Economic, Social and Cultural Rights affirms this at a global level. While IMF-imposed SAPs do not specifically require reductions to health and education budgets, such cuts usually become inevitable as part of austerity packages that force governments to slash public spending. In many countries of the global South, this reality manifests as a systemic lack of compassion towards women and girls because it is they who are largely responsible for childcare and childrearing and for the overall health and daily care of their families, including the sick and elderly. Under most austerity programs, the prices of household items and foodstuffs generally rise without a corresponding increase in incomes, and this leads to changes in household diet, impacting family nutrition and particularly affecting children, breastfeeding women and expectant mothers. Additionally, cuts to public expenditure in health and education have resulted in families being charged for some health and education services that were previously provided free of charge. And during family financial crises, girls are often the first to be pulled out of school to help at home.

Another example of the lack of compassion inherent in economic globalization is evident in indigenous communities throughout the global North and South where people, animals and nature are forced to endure what are euphemistically called the 'externalities' – pollution, biodiversity loss, species loss, respiratory illnesses and other health problems, and cultural alienation caused by the breakdown of community values – that result from the operations of multinational corporations in the extractive industry. The activities of mining companies are often in conflict, sometimes violently, with local community values and belief systems that are rooted in ideas of the collective good and that are intimately linked to nature (i.e. that are rooted in a worldview that recognizes our interdependence). These values have been eloquently expressed by indigenous leaders and are captured in an oft-repeated statement (falsely attributed to Chief Seattle): 'The Earth does not belong to us, we belong to the Earth.' While this might at first glance simply appear as a quaint expression to Westerners, it reflects a profound understanding of interdependence. This approach is reflected in indigenous respect for 'Mother Earth' and in the focus in decision-making on impacts to future generations.

For a Buddhist, the question becomes: how exactly do these extractive activities undermine the notion of interdependence expressed through community values? Through my years of work with organizations such as the Atlantic Regional Solidarity Network I have witnessed how collective values – such as the request by communities to be collectively relocated when forced by mining companies to leave their villages and lands – can be seen as barriers to negotiations from the standpoint of companies. In some cases communities are forcibly displaced, in other cases individuals are bought off and dispersed to other communities. Sometimes people are forced to live near a mine and endure constant noise and dust as well as the pollution of their land and water. Meanwhile, corporate shareholders and consumers in the global North who benefit from the outputs of the extractive industry – cell phone and computer components, gasoline, heating fuel, electricity generated from coal, etc. – do not pay the costs of such ecologically and culturally destructive activities.

Using a Marxist framework, Joel Kovel develops an elaborate set of arguments to show why capitalism cannot help but be an 'enemy of nature' and why trying to explain ecological destruction by referring simply to industry, technology or science divorced from values misses the big picture. He argues that these industries and their tools are 'instruments of capital accumulation, and have been so since the beginnings of the modern world'.[8] The way in which this becomes obvious is that many innovations that have come about as responses to the environmental crisis, but that do not fit with the needs of this model of accumulation (and its powerbrokers), will not be promoted. In many cases such alternatives are actively undermined or blocked from production. The response of oil companies to the development of the electric car is just one example.[9] As we have discussed, the creativity of big industry – cigarette, sugar, meat, dairy and genetically-modified food producers come immediately to mind – in controlling access to information and in manipulating political processes is also quite astounding.

Using a Marxist framework, I have already argued that there is limited democratic participation in capitalist societies because the economy is largely controlled by a small economic elite. But, this lack of democratic participation also exists with regard to the decisions made about what technologies should be developed and what research should be supported, or even whether a particular research or technology is actually good for society. I do not mean to suggest that all capitalist research and development has been bad for society or even to suggest that there is an objective standpoint from which we can determine what is good for society. Clearly, many incredible innovations have been developed within the context of capitalist societies, but the reality is that very few people are involved in the decision-making process, and those that are tend to be rich and powerful.

But outside of a system of meaningful democratic control over decision-making, how do we decide the directions that we want our society to go in? Or how do we even recognize that choices are being made about this whether we're involved or not? The point is, and what Marxists remind us to consider, a system whose underlying logic is the accumulation of capital cannot distinguish between what is helpful and what is destructive or, as some Buddhists would say, between what to accept and what to reject. Earlier on I discussed the implications of the corporatization of higher education. Even government-funded university research has become increasingly compromised by its collaborations with profit-making institutions.[10] And sometimes wealthy donors make very explicit demands in their 'collaborations' with universities.

As Theresa Tedesco points out in an article in the *Financial Times*, 'In 2008, banking executive John Allison donated millions of dollars to 25 U.S. colleges and universities to establish programs, including a course on "The Moral Foundations of Capitalism", dedicated to the study of Ayn Rand's books and economic philosophy. As part of the controversial 10-year deal, students are required to read *Atlas Shrugged* and Adam Smith's *The Wealth of Nations*'.[11] To say that Ayn Rand is the epitome of the individualistic, uncompassionate capitalist is an understatement! When asked if it was immoral for people to prioritize human relationships, Rand replied that if people 'place such things as friendship and family ties above their own productive work, yes, then they are immoral. Friendship, family life and human relationships are not primary in a man's life'.[12]

Similarly, while peace may be desirable from an objective standpoint (very few people would argue that killing people or being killed is a good thing), Marxists such as Ellen Meiksins Wood remind us that weapons and wars generate far too much profit for peace to be taken seriously under our capitalist system.[13] This reality was reflected in the words of Grahame Russell of the NGO Rights Action in the midst of the Syrian refugee crisis,

> Syrian, Iraqi and Afghani families are fleeing by the millions, from the bombing, violence and terrorism on the ground and from above. It seems that every country that has a jet and bombs is over there bombing, and every country and everyone bombing is righteous, bombing

for freedom, for civilization, for human rights, etc. And everyone fighting back is defending themselves from tyranny, foreign invasions, discriminations and racism ... As the bombing, death and destruction go on and on, the military industrial complex is jacked on steroids. Savvy investors are betting large on war and weapons production. Armaments factories (mainly in rich, industrialized countries) are offering double overtime to keep up with the demand, turning plowshares into guns and bombs ... Stock exchanges are humming. Pension fund and private equity managers are singing along, getting bonuses ... all for more war, all for peace and righteousness.[14]

As noted earlier, the five permanent members of the United Nations Security Council – the global body responsible for maintaining peace and security in our world – are also the world's largest weapons manufacturers. The rich and powerful, who have disproportionate control over our global institutions, have ensured a global 'order' that maintains itself through violence, both physical and structural. The point here is that, as long as killing – and any other activity that causes suffering and harm – is profitable, it will continue under capitalism. And not only does capitalism depend upon violence to maintain itself, but it has proven itself completely incapable of outgrowing this addiction under liberal democratic political systems.

So we are not at the 'end of history' where liberal democracy triumphs, as political analyst Francis Fukuyama would have it; in fact, we are far from it.[15] As we have seen, many of the freedoms and privileges we enjoy in wealthy liberal democratic societies exist because other people don't have them. And what I would like to emphasize here, is that this is precisely because capitalism and its related liberal democratic political system do not hold the most influential decision-makers to account. Of course, individual capitalists themselves are not biased towards causing harm. What I have argued in these pages, and what Marx, the Dalai Lama, the current Pope, Albert Einstein (both a socialist and an admirer of Buddhism) and countless others have long argued is that the evidence suggests that their system is.[16]

Historical examples are useful in understanding how this works. When slavery made sense for capitalism, the liberal democratic political systems in wealthy nations actively supported it and crushed any attempts to question it. When apartheid in South Africa was proving profitable, the same political systems held firmly to it and sought to quash any attempts to challenge it. When formal colonialism became too expensive to manage and was no longer required to ensure ongoing access to the wealth of the colonies, only then was it allowed to collapse. In other words, only when these violent methods of exploitation were no longer profitable, or their sheer brutality was no longer required to ensure profit-making, did politicians in wealthy liberal democracies finally begin to 'listen' to critics.

Sadly, in all of these cases we see an enduring legacy of oppression and inequality. Blacks are still systemically marginalized in the United States as are many other racialized groups and it, along with South Africa, is among the world's most unequal societies. In South Africa and many other countries today, capitalism's legal corruption ensures continuing inequality. Oxfam's 2014 *Even It Up* report on global inequality points to tax loopholes as one of the biggest problems in South Africa. As the report states, 'When the most prosperous enjoy low rates and exemptions and can take advantage of tax loopholes, and when the richest can hide their money in overseas tax havens, huge holes are left in national budgets that must be filled by the rest of us, redistributing wealth upwards'.[17] Marx of course would call this, like many other aspects of our capitalist system, robbery. But, in capitalist societies, this is just business as usual.

Oxfam points out that at least 70 per cent of Fortune 500 companies have a subsidiary in a tax haven. The world's richest 'democracy' also has the dubious honour of being the world's most unequal society. In its 2015 Global Wealth Report, international financial services company Allianz found that the United States is the world's most unequal country with regard to wealth inequality. In an acknowledgement of this reality, the report refers to the United States as the 'Unequal States of America' due to the sheer size of the wealth gap.[18]

As mentioned previously, economist Thomas Piketty argues that wealth concentration, and therefore inequality – an expression of structural violence – is inherent to free-market capitalism. One of his central arguments is that the free-market system has a natural tendency towards increasing the concentration of wealth. Piketty's solutions include a global tax on capital and punitive taxes on those earning over $500,000 per year.[19] *The Economist* magazine, predictably, has problems with Piketty's focus on making the rich pay such taxes. It argues that 'Thomas Piketty's blockbuster book is a great piece of scholarship, but a poor guide to policy'.[20] Marxists of course would point out that taxation of the rich is not in reality about redistribution but is in fact a rather inadequate way of returning to the producers some of the stolen products of their labour. The fact that even Picketty's modest suggestions to build more accountability into the system are met with such responses demonstrates what we are up against in trying to democratize our economic system and establish meaningful concepts of citizenship. After all, Pickety's policy measures, though radical when measured against current policy-making, would leave capitalism intact. In actuality, and when we look at citizenship from a global perspective and in the context of global capitalism, we realize the need to establish a systemic alternative that would blend the radical democracy of genuine socialism with the compassion and wisdom called for by Buddhists. After all, we cannot call a system democratic when it is a system that is dependent on upholding violence internationally, a system where the most important decisions are not made by the people, a system in which a minority control most of the wealth while a majority of the world's population lives in poverty and, finally, a system under which the very survival of our planet is threatened.

Despite the democratic deficit, the great creativity and seductive power of consumer capitalism – presented as the

Western development model – continues to fuel the dreams of people around the world even though there is hard evidence that most people are not going to benefit from it in any significant way. In fact, most people cannot benefit given the finite nature of the planet we live on. But not only will most people not enjoy Western living standards, many of them will have to endure ongoing economic austerity. Our economic leaders have been very effective in making the bitter medicine of austerity seem necessary and ultimately beneficial. In fact, organizations such as the World Bank have worked hard to incorporate the notion of participation into their programs. The rather clever idea is to get people to actively participate in carrying out their own austerity programs. But, in no way does participation allow for either questioning the basis of these programs or their ultimate agenda.

In a global economic environment of dog-eat-dog competitiveness, all countries are 'encouraged' to make themselves as attractive as possible to foreign investors by reducing the barriers to trade and investment. But what does that mean in practice? As any good Marxist knows, it means that structurally, those leaders and institutions guiding the process ('advanced' capitalist countries, multinational corporations, the IMF, the World Bank and the WTO) must advocate for the free movement of capital and goods – but *not* workers. In effect, they must advocate for the extensive rights of powerful economic actors, particularly corporations, to intervene in the political processes and to benefit from the natural resources and cheap labour in communities and countries where they are not citizens. But if workers attempt to cross borders to improve their lot, they face all kinds of barriers, legal and physical.

The global North has not been immune to economic globalization and its related austerity agenda. In recent decades, many wealthy nations have experienced cuts in public spending, the privatization of state-owned companies, and deregulation. However, in the global North, these reforms have not been imposed on us by unelected international institutions but rather by our own elected governments. Furthermore, our deeper social safety nets, credit cards and continued exploitation of the global South have so far allowed us to survive much of the socioeconomic fallout.

Looking at the business news in the mainstream media makes it very obvious that this free trade and austerity approach is simply seen as part of the 'common sense' of contemporary capitalism. In sharp contrast, it is very interesting and politically significant to see how those arguing for a globalization that recognizes our interdependence and celebrates our diversity, that promotes locally-based economies or the freer movement of people between countries or the inclusion of other species or the environment into debates on democracy and citizenship have to jump through extensive interpersonal, political and theoretical hoops to justify their efforts.

But, as I have shown throughout this book, because most decision-making elites are not held accountable under any form of meaningful democratic process, inequality and a lack of compassion manifest not only in a lack of economic wellbeing but also in the harms that arise through discrimination along race, ethnic, religious and gender lines. For instance, people from the global South face all sorts of restrictions when they attempt to travel to wealthy nations, either to improve their lives or even just to take a vacation. And yet economic elites – and most citizens of global North countries – can travel freely to almost every corner of the globe. In fact, anyone from a wealthy nation who has ever travelled in the global South, and was paying attention, would have quickly noticed how easy it was for them to move around the world, particularly if they are white and not of Middle Eastern descent.

Structural violence is visible in the everyday practices at embassies, airports and borders where the lighter your skin and the fuller your wallet, the more rights you have, even just the right not to be bothered. An Indian student of mine who has been living in Canada for several years and whose English is immaculate, recently shared in class that he has *never* travelled internationally without being either questioned or searched or both at an airport. His white Canadian classmates were duly shocked.

The important thing about this discrimination is the significance behind such inequality. It is the structural manifestation of the denial of our interdependence. Money and the wealth it represents becomes the medium of value and the source of division. In practice, citizens of the global North – and to some degree elites in the global South – are treated as though they possess greater value as people. Most citizens of the world do not travel freely unless they have lots of money. The long queues at US embassies in countries throughout Latin

America as people hope to obtain a visa provide a glimpse into this reality. There are extensive hoops to jump through.

The US government is, of course, very aware of this system that it has helped to create and, therefore, grants citizens of Cuba the right to instant US residency upon arrival in the United States. The propaganda value of saying that citizens are leaving Cuba because socialism does not work has been too powerful a tool to pass up. But for Mexicans and Central Americans who are suffering greatly from policies directly connected to corporate capitalism, a monstrous border wall is being built to keep them out.[21] The fact that so many Mexicans, Salvadorans and Guatemalans want to leave their homelands apparently does not reflect negatively on capitalism, but Cubans leaving their country represents the failure of socialism.

I have shown how a Marxist view demonstrates the limited nature of democracy within 'advanced' capitalist countries, revealing how it does not extend in any meaningful way to the work environments that most of us inhabit or to the broader economic system. But viewing the terrain of democracy more globally makes this problem all the more visible. It becomes immediately evident that some of the core values we associate, however problematically and ideologically, with countries that have long liberal democratic traditions – the capacity to influence the decisions that impact our lives and the right to be treated as equal citizens (i.e. our wealth should have nothing to do with our capacity to exercise our rights) – are not only compromised under capitalism, their violation is part-and-parcel of the system.

Everywhere that economic reforms have been implemented in the global South there has been resistance and protest. And these 'reforms', what Marxists would identify as the latest round of imperialist policies, are being imposed on the South not because leaders of those nations are disproportionately poor at balancing budgets or because their citizens are lazier than us. It is, as Marxists tell us, because the entire global capitalist economy has been built to serve the interests of particular countries and international economic elites. For decades, as part of corporate globalization, global North governments have been imposing Structural Adjustment Programs on the South – often with the cooperation of elites in the South – in order to pry open their borders to access their cheap labour, natural resources and markets, and to force them to focus on economic growth with the promise that they can become like us.

The overwhelming majority of people in the global South have no democratic voice in this process. These are authoritarian decisions imposed on them by the governments of wealthy nations, multinational corporations and inter-national institutions. But what would it look like if the tables were turned on us? What if the nations of the global South possessed the power to force us to live more sustainably and compassionately?

Imagine you have walked into a room where a global summit of world decision-makers is occurring, but there is something very different about this gathering. Imagine that the spirit of this meeting reflects the socialist and Buddhist values that have been highlighted throughout this book, a process where the voices of the marginalized are heard, where the harms of the global capitalist system are acknowledged, where global interdependence is recognized and where a compassionate citizenship is promoted. On one side of the table are the usual suspects, representatives of international financial institutions such as the IMF and the World Bank as well as those from governments and corporations based in wealthy nations. On the other side are leaders from the global South who have been democratically elected by their citizens. There are three features of the global economic order that inform the content of this 'negotiation' process: the fragile state of the planet's ecosystem, the proliferation of violence including state and sub-state terrorism, and the failure of Western nations to take into account the human rights and ecological impacts and global reach of their consumer lifestyles.

In this hypothetical example, countries of the global North are now being obligated to engage in a Structural Adjustment Program to ensure a more equitable global distribution of the planet's resources and to safeguard the future of the planet itself. Given the sheer magnitude of the problems identified and the global North's inability to effectively address them, the global South group sees no alternative but to impose reforms on their northern counterparts. Therefore, the reason for this meeting is not to negotiate a solution, but for the global South representatives to simply go over the basic terms of the agreement and lay out the timeline that the global North must adhere to.

The meeting begins with a brief presentation from a representative of the global South contingent:

> We live in an interdependent world and under globalization that world has become much smaller. The connections that we have to each other, to other species and to nature by virtue of our existence on this planet are ever more visible to us. This should be a cause for joy, a reason to appreciate, share and celebrate the differences and beauty of our diverse cultures, animals and lands. But instead we are confronted by wars that we can't seem to end, by the abuse and destruction of many species and by the increasing likelihood of ecological collapse. I think we all understand the regrettable circumstances that have led to today's meeting. We have tried on numerous occasions to raise the issue of overconsumption and to curb the fundamentalism and ruthlessness with which the growth economy and austerity have been promoted in recent years.
>
> Many of you will remember the courageous attempts to raise these issues that came about under the guise of the New International Economic Order (NIEO) in the late 1970s. The NIEO was a call from the global South for an international system that could create space for genuine democracy and to allow self-reliance to emerge in whatever form deemed appropriate, including democratic socialism, in our various regions. After the debt crisis of the 1980s this call was silenced by the onslaught of IMF

structural adjustment programs throughout the so-called Third World.

Many of us here come from the Third World or, as it is also euphemistically called, the 'developing world'. In fact, most of humanity lives in the Third World. Our indigenous brothers and sisters have the dubious honour of being referred to as the 'Fourth World'. More and more of us are confused about when the so-called 'developing' nations will become the 'developed' nations. And, what is this 'development' thing anyway? Do we actually want it? As most of you have probably noticed, more than 500 years after the so-called 'civilizing' mission of colonialism, the same number of years of capitalism and, more recently, over 30 years of corporate globalization, the majority of us are still very firmly ensconced in the Third World.

The pockets of our populations now enjoying Western lifestyles are in the minority and all of us have seen the devastating consequences of the penetration of Western consumer culture into our societies – from increasing inequality to environmental devastation to increasing levels of depression and to alarming increases in industrial diseases. We do not reject Western culture *per se*. For one thing, we're not sure what it is and, even if we did know, it is not our business to tell anyone else how to live as long as it does not harm us.

What we have raised our voices against is the authoritarian presence of capitalist corporate interests in our countries and the homogenizing penetration of capitalist consumer culture into so many spheres of our lives. This penetration has been rooted in the exploitation of our peoples' labour, land and resources. In many of our communities this has led to the complete devastation of our cultural fabric. And last but definitely not least, the disproportionate contribution of rich capitalist countries to environmental destruction and global warming has made it decisively clear that entirely new global systems of accountability must be put into place. We simply have no choice.

We acknowledge that the wealthy and powerful in our countries have often supported colonialism and neo-colonialism and this is why so many of them have been removed from power in recent years. And for those who haven't, and are not present here, we now also want to call them to account. The fact is that today we are faced with unrelenting global violence and what some see as a possibly irreversible environmental catastrophe that we believe only extreme austerity measures applied to the North can address. We have tried to come up with a timeline that will make the transition to a more peaceful and sustainable global economy as painless as possible but we also acknowledge that there will inevitably be disharmony and possible political protest accompanying these reform measures. Several years ago, former economist for the World Bank, Joseph Stiglitz, coined the term 'IMF riot', which was used to determine the threshold of how far an economy could be pushed before citizens would revolt. As karma would have it, we may end up having to use a similar strategy with regard to pushing the rich countries of the global North towards a saner and more compassionate world.

Some groups feeding into the democratic process informing this advisory group have argued that it is simply the culture of the North, and of whites in particular, to over-consume and to wage war to protect their interests, and that they 'just don't like our sustainable ways'. Nevertheless, the advisory group insists that an open and inclusive education process could begin to deal with what some have called 'these backward ways of thinking'. And while we realize the need for integrated actions with regard to building genuine democracy globally and confronting head on the current violence being perpetrated around the world, the key focus of these austerity measures will be an immediate reduction in overall consumption in global North countries. This will necessarily have import-export implications because many northern firms are invested in global South countries that provide cheap consumer goods to the North.

The reduction in consumption will be measured according to global per capita ecological footprint figures where global North countries will have a timeline to bring their consumption in line with sustainable global footprint numbers. In other words, countries from the global North would only use, in a sustainable manner, a share of the planet's resources in proportion to their share of the world's population. For example, if the US population amounts to four per cent of the world's population, then the United States has a right to consume four per cent of the planet's resources. We believe that there is no alternative to this approach. Thank you for listening and I hope we are successful in building a saner, more sustainable and compassionate world.

While structural adjustment imposed on the global North by the global South is not likely to happen in the near future – nor is it desirable because citizens of the global North should have the right to a voice in the decisions that impact their lives – pondering the possibility even for a moment highlights the greed and arrogance of the narrative and practices of our current global economic elites as well as the authoritarianism of their decision-making under global capitalism.

It is an authoritarianism that allows multinational corporations to exploit the cheap labour and natural resources of the global South. And it co-exists with an arrogance that demands nations in the global South shift to liberal democratic forms of governance and tackle poverty with the few resources they have left. But what becomes clear is that our current ideas and practices of democracy, which do not extend to the economic sphere and do not take into consideration the realities of global economic relationships, are both an expression of structural violence and a barrier to creating a more sane, ecologically sustainable and compassionate world.

It is the lack of transparency and accountability under capitalism that allows for the routine exploitation of people, non-human animals and nature, because there are no effective systems in place to prevent it. The arguments that I have made here point to the fact that capitalism and democracy are not compatible if our idea of democracy extends to economic activity (in the form of worker and community-owned cooperatives, for example) and beyond borders in order to provide everyone impacted by policies a voice in determining those policies. Taking this broader view of democracy, a view that recognizes our interdependence in all spheres, allows us to make visible the interconnected nature of various forms of exploitation. These issues go to the heart of our system of government and our role as citizens of a global community. What would be the features and values of a global system that takes interdependence seriously? It is to this question that I will turn in the next chapter.

CHAPTER 7

IN SEARCH OF THE GLOBAL CITIZEN

Today, more than ever before, life must be characterized by a sense of universal responsibility, not only nation to nation and human to human, but also human to other forms of life.

— The Dalai Lama

It is time to explore how our ideas about citizenship and democracy are fundamental to the possibilities of moving beyond the suffering, greed and delusion of our capitalist system. We need to reflect on the understandable resentment that many around the world may feel about being constantly thought of as 'less developed' while their resources are simultaneously being exploited to feed the consumption habits of the 'developed' nations. In conversations about the 'Third' and 'Fourth' worlds, we often hear the refrain, 'If *those* people could just get their shit together, they wouldn't have so much poverty and violence'. But, as we have seen, examining the global picture reveals a much more complicated story.

Looking at this as citizens from the global North, and with a view of interdependence in mind, we need to acknowledge our daily complicity in this system, not only as beneficiaries of globalized corporate capitalism but also as citizens of countries with disproportionate wealth and decision-making power. And when we seek to simply blame the military-industrial complex, corporate CEOs, or the IMF and World Bank, Buddhists would remind us that the reality of our interdependence means that it is not just about some 'evil oppressor' out there. As cartoonist Walt Kelly's 1970 Earth Day poster stated, 'We Have Met The Enemy and He Is Us'.[1] And this is because, as Sakyong Mipham has noted,

> At this time, materialism and its consumeristic influence over every aspect of our lives is an invisible totalitarian regime. However, unlike previous totalitarian regimes, this regime is omnipresent, and we are all participating. If we think it's impossible to create enlightened society, that's a sign we've been so thoroughly convinced by this system that we can no longer visualize an alternative. Our minds have grown small with fixation on consumption as a means to satisfaction.[2]

So while corporate CEOs and other global economic elites largely control the agenda-making process, it is up to each one of us to acknowledge our place in this system and to determine what we should do, including calling our so-called leaders to account and mounting challenges to the system itself. Clearly, it is not about providing charity (small c compassion), it will require massive restructuring of our economic system (to reflect big C compassion) by moving towards an alternative, more compassionate and sustainable social system. Such a global society would be marked by democratic processes that affirm mutuality, horizontality and respect as well as recognize our interdependence as the various cultures, races, religions, species and ecosystems sharing this planet.

This process could begin with getting our own ship in order instead of trying to control and manipulate everybody else's boats to serve our own purposes. And, as I have argued, it is not about making privileged people in the global North feel guilty because that's not particularly helpful nor is it the point. We might just need to get past feeling guilty and get on with making things better. As I have argued throughout this book, bringing about change involves first acknowledging the harms suffered – so we can begin pulling out arrows – and recognizing the institutional and structural framework that perpetuates this suffering. Part of that process is rethinking how decisions are made within our workplaces, communities and societies, and at a global level.

To seriously tackle the suffering and alienation that socialists and Buddhists identify as part of the daily reality of our world today, we have to build a global citizenship that has at its foundation the 'sense of universal responsibility' that the Dalai Lama speaks of in the quotation at the beginning of this chapter. This is not a fluffy idea; it has quite practical implications. It is, in some ways, revolutionary in that it implies a fundamental transformation of our current ways of living as a global community. We would actually have to become one! It speaks not only to how we structure our political and economic institutions but to the values we need to cultivate in ourselves and our children. No matter how creative our rules and procedures, our institutions and processes, or how beautifully crafted our constitutions, none of this means much, nor will it protect us from doing harm, if our revolution is not guided by people deeply committed to values.

Marxist revolutionary Ernesto 'Che' Guevara once said, 'At the risk of seeming ridiculous, let me say that the true revolutionary is guided by a great feeling of love. It is impossible to think of a genuine revolutionary lacking this quality'.[3] I believe this great feeling of love is expressed in the understanding of our fundamental interdependence as human beings: with each other, with other animals and with nature. And this love has at its root an orientation towards compassion. As Shambhala Buddhist teacher Moh Hardin says, 'Sometimes thinking about love (wishing happiness) is appropriate; at other times it is more appropriate to think about compassion (freedom from suffering). It is good to cultivate both of them, for they go hand in hand'.[4]

In order to get to a place where we can develop a global citizenship, and societies guided by these values, we have to first understand the values guiding our current processes of decision-making, both nationally and internationally, and why they are not working for us. We know they don't work for all the reasons I have outlined in this book: widespread poverty; inequality; ecological degradation; authoritarianism; and ongoing violence, both structural and physical, experienced by humans and other animals. But a fundamental problem arises when we begin thinking about establishing a saner and more compassionate global citizenship and how it relates to the nature of our contemporary democracies. When we look globally we see a huge democratic deficit for most of the world's population. That is, most people around the world have no voice in the major decisions (and often even in the minor decisions) that affect their lives. As Bill Martin points out, 'When Marx talked about "class dictatorship" so long ago, what people seem to miss, and that needs to be driven home once again, is that there is a ruling class, and this class operates according to certain imperatives. Simply put, and on one level it is just this simple, in the United States and for pretty much the whole world, *capital decides*.'[5]

Governments in the global South have found themselves forced to respond and adapt to the demands of powerful outside forces – governments of wealthy nations, multinational corporations and international institutions – that dominate the global economic system rather than to the interests of their own populations. This is because we have nothing resembling a global democratic decision-making process that corresponds with the global economic reality of corporate capitalism. Therefore, it would seem that global citizenship implies global democracy. And while I do think we need to build completely new global institutions, I would argue that building genuine democracies closer to home – that consider the wellbeing of other societies, species and nature – is a good place to start.

While it is generally accepted in theory – although not often in practice – that people should have rights and agency as citizens, we have yet to take into consideration how our foreign policy and Northern-dominated global economic institutions affect the capacity of citizens in the global South to exercise their democratic rights, never mind considering the impacts of this framework on their overall wellbeing. Universal responsibility would require that we see these things as fundamental aspects of how we measure the success of our own democracies. In the same way that we would not generally define someone as a kind person if after being incredibly caring to their own family they exit the house to beat other people up. And, as I have argued throughout this book, we certainly have not properly incorporated other species and the environment into our existing democratic frameworks.

And yet the mainstream view is that Canada, the United States, the UK and other global North countries are democratic. The fact that this is generally believed is largely because of the way we measure democracy. In the West, when we measure the democratic credentials of particular countries, we tend to refer to the kinds of criteria used by the US-based Freedom House or the Austria-based Democracy Ranking Association. Under these rankings it is implied that democracies are 'electoral' (involving multiparty elections) and 'liberal' (prioritizing a wide array of individual civil liberties over collective rights). And there are certainly no criteria to determine how 'fair' or democratic a country's foreign policy is as part of the determination of its democratic credentials. This limited view is ultimately a problem under economic globalization, particularly when we try to express universal responsibility and the compassion that this entails.

At the level of individual consciousness, both Marxists and socially-engaged Buddhists remind us how the values reinforced by the capitalist system – individualism, greed, materialism, wastefulness, competition, etc. – are at the root of our suffering. Marxists also remind us that we are kidding ourselves if we believe we can ignore the relationship between democracy and our systems of production and consumption. In this vein, socialists of all colours point to the incredible significance of how we determine 'value', particularly the value of labour as key to our struggle to liberate ourselves from oppression and suffering and to work towards genuinely democratic societies. This means that as a society we need to reflect on how decisions about production are made and what the impacts of those decisions are with regard to genuine democracy and citizen wellbeing both within our own societies and globally.

At an individual level it means reflecting on and questioning what we do as work and how we relate to our work (feeling it is meaningful, having a sense of purpose, expressing individual creativity, etc.), how our work is organized (democratic, inclusive and safe workplaces), and how we relate to the work of others (they are not means to our ends, we share with them broader social goals and values, our collaborations are guided by respect and promote dignity). All of the forms of suffering and alienation explored in this book suggest that this reflection is a necessary part of the process of redesigning the future in the direction of social justice. However, even just looking at one of the problems discussed here – such as global warming –

it is almost impossible to imagine achieving the desired goals, and in most contexts even effectively working towards them, within a capitalist framework.[6]

Buddhist notions of interdependence, the related idea of universal responsibility and big C compassion would suggest that we need to create systems where *all* forms of oppression against humans, other animals and nature become impossible or at least very difficult, and where extreme inequality in wealth would not be structurally possible. Hence, as Marxists would suggest, we need to overthrow the capitalist system! The overthrow of capitalism is necessary not because all capitalists are people of ill will or bad intention, but rather because an oppressive logic is built into the system of capital accumulation and no matter how much friendlier we can make it in particular contexts, we can never overcome this fundamental logic.

Of course many books could be written to determine what such a revolution might look like practically. Here I would simply like to suggest that at a basic level we are deciding moment to moment how to engage or disengage from this logic and, if we are guided by the 'right view' we are likely to act from a place of compassion. As I have argued in these pages, the revolution might begin with our refusal as individuals and as communities to participate in some of the worst aspects of our system. In other words, to stop contributing to harm. This is what people in progressive social movements around the world are attempting to do by constructing community alternatives, by defending the rights of humans and other animals, by working in solidarity with communities around the world who share their values (including liberation from oppressions of race, gender and sexuality) and, in the short term, by lobbying governments and international institutions to implement change. Building more intentional, compassionate and inclusive economic systems is not the only answer to the suffering of humans and other animals, but because our very survival depends on our ability to reproduce ourselves in the natural world (which requires that we produce and consume), then Marxists have justifiably identified it as absolutely fundamental.

So, what Marxism makes clear is that our discussions about democracy and citizenship should never be divorced from our discussions of production (our economic system) and, therefore, of labour. And Buddhism reminds us that to end suffering, alternative systems should be guided by a view that acknowledges our interdependence with all beings and nature and, therefore, be rooted in compassion. So how might alternative systems that we create feed into promoting the kinds of values we want to live by? Can we conceive of genuinely compassionate democracies that respect the dignity of humans and other animals and the ecological integrity of the natural world? And do we accept the 'universal responsibility' that these things imply?

In speaking of universal responsibility, the Dalai Lama highlights not only the need to confront the immediate 'ignorance, greed, and lack of respect for the earth's living things' that our current systems and behaviours reflect, but he also suggests our responsibility reaches far into the future. While our ancestors may be forgiven for not grasping the finite nature of our planet's resources, we have no excuse. As the Dalai Lama points out, 'It is essential that we re-examine ethically what we have inherited, what we are responsible for, and what we will pass on to coming generations. Clearly this is a pivotal generation'.[7]

The challenge then, is not to attempt to integrate ethics into the already existing system, but to actually turn the current system on its head. As noted above, the first step in this process is for people guided by the values of interdependence and compassion to make visible the interconnected nature of various forms of oppression – which could involve variations on the 'bodies in the basement' approach. Acknowledging the bodies in the basement is the first stage of bringing transparency to the system so we can more clearly see what's wrong with the way things are. It is at this stage where we become socially engaged and where we confront entrenched beliefs and values.

An acknowledgement of all the harms caused by the current system allows us to see that solutions require a new approach to reaching our social goals, an entirely new way of thinking about production and consumption. And this new approach would reach for an inclusivity in our political and economic systems that cuts across race, class, gender, animal and nature frameworks as well as transcending the traditional boundaries of the nation-state.

A number of scholars have pointed out the challenges inherent in liberal democratic approaches to citizenship when applied to twenty-first century problems, particularly flagging modern concepts of national identity. David Held, for example, in his call for 'cosmopolitanism', argues that our ideas of democracy have been too narrowly focused and haven't recognized what he calls 'overlapping communities of fate'.[8] From a different angle, while generally sympathetic to the Western liberal democratic model, citizenship scholar Richard Bellamy argues that we've had a tendency to try to squeeze cultures and communities that extend across regions into the nation-state framework. According to Bellamy,

> while state-building and nation-building went hand in hand in the past, there are obvious problems in drawing too tight a connection between the two. It is estimated that there are between 5,000 and 9,000 ethnic-cultural groups in the world, and only around 200 states, over 90% of which contain more than one ethnic group. To overcome this diversity, nation-building in the past involved some or all of the following: genocide, forced mass-population transfers, coerced assimilation, and domination and control by the ruling group.[9]

Meanwhile, in her exploration of the significance of 'place' in ecological theory, Val Plumwood frames the problem as 'dematerialization', by which she means our 'remoteness from ecological consequences and illusions of our independence of nature and of the irrelevance of nature'.[10] Therefore, the void in responsibility and accountability that currently exists needs be filled with a new interconnected approach to citizenship that includes humans, other animals and nature.

A further challenge that Marxists and other socialists point out is that liberal democracy has historically been associated with capitalism; therefore, it has been rooted in the separation of the political and economic spheres. This has meant that democracy exists to varying degrees in the political sphere (depending on which country you're looking at) but, as I have argued in this book, it is generally very limited in the economic sphere where it tends to be reduced to state regulation (e.g. setting standards around things like food labelling, worker's rights or environmental regulations for companies) and welfare policies. The degree to which there is no real expectation of genuine democratic accountability in the economy is demonstrated quite visibly in the 'Democracy Ranking', which prioritizes democracy in the political sphere far more than in the economic sphere – and there is certainly no suggestion that influential economic decision-makers such as corporate CEOs should be elected.[11]

Given the systemic nature of the problem and the structural violence that it entails, it is clear that establishing meaningful citizenship requires taking a structural approach, in other words, an approach that reflects our interdependence. This does not mean we throw out the idea of bounded communities that remain committed to place and culture, but rather it calls for an approach that recognizes the reality that there are communities, institutions and individuals in certain nations acting in ways that impact humans, other animals and nature in other communities and nations.

The notion of a citizenship based on interdependence is a somewhat countercultural idea in the global North to the degree that it requires a worldview that is in opposition to the logic and parameters of Western capitalist societies. Interconnected citizenship contradicts the individualistic, linear, progress and growth-oriented ideology that fuels the capitalist economy. But a number of perspectives and movements have emerged in both the global North and the global South in recent years that point to interconnected citizenship. Interesting links can be drawn between eco-socialist approaches, indigenous perspectives and social movements in the North and South. Often in the view of these movements there is a focus on the idea of the 'commons' and the fact that the exploitation of humans, non-human animals and nature has occurred through the systematic enclosure and exploitation of once commonly-held lands.

Large-scale production for profit requires systematic dis-placement of peoples from their lands, and the commodifi-cation of animals and resources goes hand-in-hand with this process. Historically this was often seen as part of the 'civilizing' process without which modern progress could not occur. Marx called this process 'primitive accumulation' in which 'The expropriation of the agricultural producer, of the peasant, from the soil, is the basis of the whole [capitalist] process. The history of this expropriation assumes different aspects in different countries, and runs through its various phases in different orders of succession, and at different historical epochs'.[12]

The process of privatizing and commodifying the commons continues today under corporate globalization as theorists and communities struggle to form counter-narratives and movements. From the eco-socialist angle, and echoing indigenous philosophy, Joel Kovel argues that the idea of property is central to the problem of exploitation:

> Taken all in all, the earth we inhabit should be regarded, not as our collective property but as a wondrous matrix from which we emerge and to which we return ... Indeed, ownership of the planet is a pathetic illusion. It is plain hubris to think that the earth, or nature, can be owned – and stupid to boot, as though one can own that which gives us being, and whose becoming we express.[13]

Meanwhile, authors such as Meiksins Wood, Kovel, Leech, Nibert and others draw on a Marxist framework to call for a truly participatory and more compassionate democratic socialism, as opposed to the centralized, authoritarian and ecologically-destructive model epitomized by the Soviet Union in the twentieth century. Such a system would involve the emancipation of both humans and nature based on a *usufructuary* relationship to nature (the idea that you can use nature but not own it and abuse it) and social (versus private) ownership of the means of production. For Kovel, the 'eco' in eco-socialism is particularly important because any democratic system divorced from nature will always leave nature vulnerable and ultimately prove to be unsustainable.

A key part of this perspective is the idea that nature, like the humans and other animals that are part of it, has an intrinsic value. As Kovel explains, 'The precondition of an ecologically rational attitude toward nature is the recognition that nature far surpasses us and has its own intrinsic value, irreducible to our practice'.[14] Similarly, notes David Nibert,

> A socialist system is one in which the important resources and key production technology and facilities are owned by members of the society and used for their collective benefit. A socialist system would be characterized by democratic decision-making and the development of strong and much more egalitarian communities. It is in the context of such a social system that liberty, equality, and fraternity, a reversal of environmental destruction and the reduction of oppression of humans and other animals could be realized.[15]

In other words, if we recognize the intrinsic value of nature, as Buddhists constantly remind us to do, then our decisions about how to use it for our 'collective benefit' will always be made through this lens. In alignment with this view, the forms of 'productive activity', and the ways in which we collectively decide how these forms will work, are central questions in the construction of a more expansive, interdependent and compassionate democracy. For Marxists and socially-engaged Buddhists, this means recognizing value – in nature and people – beyond the reductionist idea of 'exchange value' that exists under capitalism. As Kovel suggests, it is crucial that we recognize 'ecosystemic integrity' in our society, 'whether this be the raising of beautiful children, the growing of organic gardens, the playing of excellent string quartets, the cleaning of streets, the making of composting toilets, or the invention of new technologies for turning solar energy into fuel cells'.[16]

It would take a much longer book than this to do justice to the numerous examples of individuals and communities across the globe that are engaged in social justice movements and projects that reflect alternative approaches to citizenship.[17] My more modest goal here is to identify a few interesting and important examples of alternative perspectives that, while not necessarily defined as Buddhist or Marxist, reflect many of the Buddhist and Marxist perspectives presented in this book. In particular, they emphasize the kinds of values and social goals that acknowledge our global interdependence as living beings and our connection to the planet.

Indian philosopher and activist Vandana Shiva has proposed a system of 'Earth Democracy', which is being implemented in numerous rural communities in India and is grounded in the idea of the interconnectedness of everything on this planet. Shiva does not self-identify as a Marxist, but she has been identified by Marxist Ian Angus as 'an authentic and powerful voice of Third World opposition to capitalist ecocide'.[18] And while Shiva is also not a Buddhist, she received the Right Livelihood award in 1993 in recognition of her advocacy for a more compassionate world so, in this sense, she is an example of the universality of the values I have been discussing throughout this book.

Her concept of 'Earth Democracy', which is rooted in compassion, focuses on the reclaiming of the commons as crucial to ending corporate globalization and the 'cultures of exclusion, dispossession, and scarcity' that it creates. In a similar vein to eco-socialists, Shiva argues that the reduction of all beings and resources to commodities 'robs diverse species and people of their rightful share of ecological, cultural and economic, and political space'.[19] She argues that capitalism and its industrial models of mass production have been at the centre of the destruction of indigenous systems of production and knowledge and the destruction of diversity in humans (culture, language, diet, etc.), other species and plants. According to Shiva,

> All beings are subjects who have integrity, intelligence, and identity, not objects of ownership, manipulation, exploitation, or disposability ... We are all members of the earth family, interconnected through the planet's fragile web of life. We all have a duty to live in a manner that protects the earth's ecological processes, and the rights and welfare of all species and all people. No humans have the right to encroach on the ecological space of other species and other people, or to treat them with cruelty and violence.[20]

Shiva also cleverly interweaves the idea of the homogenizing effects of capitalist penetration into non-Western cultures with the idea that capitalism has been instrumental in creating, not only ecologically-destructive monocultures of nature, but mentally and spiritually destructive 'monocultures of the mind'. These monocultures of the mind are perhaps the most profound expression of the fundamental alienation at the root of our economic system. At a very practical level, and contrary to the Western narrative, she is suggesting that genuinely democratic systems cannot bypass culture or nature because respect for these two realms and their inherent diversity is fundamental to its realization. But respecting culture and nature cannot simply be about bringing token communities into discussions as 'stakeholders' or as afterthoughts. It is first about orienting ourselves towards a big C compassion view of suffering, which includes recognizing and responding to the fact that humans, other species and nature are affected by structural violence.

Shiva has devised simple yet profound principles for Earth Democracy based on living economies and living cultures. As Shiva states, 'Earth Democracy evolves from the consciousness that while we are rooted locally we are also connected to the world as a whole, and, in fact, to the entire universe'.[21] There are ten principles of Earth Democracy:

1. All species, peoples, and cultures have intrinsic worth;
2. The earth community is a democracy of all life;
3. Diversity in nature and culture must be defended;
4. All beings have a natural right to sustenance;
5. Earth Democracy is based on living economies and economic democracy;
6. Living economies are built on local economies;
7. Earth democracy is a living democracy;

8. Earth Democracy is based on living cultures;

9. Living cultures are life nourishing;

10. Earth Democracy globalizes peace, care and compassion.[22]

While all of these principles are incredibly important I will focus on Shiva's second and tenth principles because they imply a global citizenship that recognizes the interdependence of all beings and nature. For Shiva and others, including the New Economy Movement discussed earlier in this book, realizing the values that these principles are rooted in involves 'localizing' decision-making and production systems as much as possible. Not only is this more empowering for individual citizens, but it ensures that protection of the earth is a primary concern in all decision-making. Her perspective recognizes that not all goods can be derived locally, but the point is to achieve this wherever possible. With this in mind, Shiva pays particular attention to the primacy of food self-reliance which, she argues, is at the root of community resilience.

This approach is evident in the Navdanya Movement (Nine Seed Movement), which works across seventeen states in India with a focus on seed and food sovereignty. With regard to animals, it is a movement that, while not eliminating the use of animals for food, calls for an end to cruelty and factory farming.[23] Navdanya describes itself as a 'network of seed keepers and organic producers' and Shiva herself, as a leader in the movement, has emphasized the significance of the seed as the root of all life: human, animal and plant. The patenting and ownership of plant seed under the current intellectual property rights regime of the WTO, she argues, is painfully symbolic of the degree to which capitalist ownership has penetrated even the basis of life itself, thereby violating the very foundation of the commons.[24] To return to a theme from the beginning of this book, when the very seeds of life are 'thingified', we witness one of capitalism's most profound violations.

Navdanya is an important movement for many reasons but key to these is its emphasis on building a decentralized, democratic and sustainable food system based on the principles of Earth Democracy. The movement clearly reflects the principles of interdependence that I have been discussing throughout this book but with an Indian flavour. The Navdanya movement echoes the calls of Mahatma Gandhi for *Swaraj*, which means sovereignty, but in this case referring to sovereignty in terms of seed, food, water and land. In reference to its origins, the organization states, 'Navdanya started the Earth Democracy movement, which provides an alternative worldview in which humans are embedded in the Earth Family, we are connected to each other through love, compassion, not hatred and violence and ecological responsibility and economic justice replaces greed, consumerism and competition as objectives of human life'.[25]

The IMF, the World Bank, the WTO and multinational corporations have pressured the Indian government, and many other governments in the global South, into selling off the commons to the highest bidder. As Navdanya notes, 'The entry of companies like Cargill into direct procurements, transportation and processing is leading to the closure of small local and larger agro-processing units that provide livelihoods to lots of people. We demand that food be accepted as a Fundamental Human Right and is produced and distributed in a democratic manner'.[26] India is not unique in this aspect. Many authors, and Marxists in particular, have noted that the enclosure of the commons has long been a feature of capitalist development, historically implemented by robber barons and colonizing powers, now facilitated by economic 'reforms' promoted by the IMF and World Bank as well as within the WTO and regional trade agreements. All of these institutions protect the undemocratic access of foreign corporations to the resources and markets of global South countries such as India.

Capitalist corporations not only seek to impose Westernized industrial agriculture on India and other nations of the global South but also unhealthy Western diets through what a Marxist might call 'food imperialism'. When I was in India recently, I asked a hotel manager to suggest a restaurant for dinner one evening. He explained how a vibrant shopping area had emerged in the neighbourhood and that I could easily find McDonalds and Pizza Hut just around the corner. He seemed surprised and mildly pleased to discover that I was in fact looking for Indian, and specifically vegan, options. A young Navdanya worker explained to me that in her town the 'cool' kids ate at KFC and drank Coca-Cola, and that places like McDonalds were seen as the hip hangouts. She explained that traditional Indian food, while far superior in terms of diversity of choice, nutritional content and support for Indian producers (all factors effectively addressed by Navdanya), was seen by many of her peers as inferior. She said that it was only when her boyfriend began challenging her on her Western dietary choices that she became interested in learning more about capitalist food systems and the insidious promotion of junk food diets in the global South. She is now working for Navdanya to promote organic agriculture and healthier eating in India and was recently caught by relatives pouring Coca-Cola down the sink at a family party.

The Earth Democracy movement in general, and Navdanya in particular, are important for our arguments here because they tap into the centrality – and universality – of land and food for both democracy and the environment. While specific issues in communities around the world will differ, as will the appropriate responses, the overall problems are shared. The global capitalist food system not only infringes on peoples' rights to land and food but, as Shiva notes, it also ensures the ongoing 'overexploitation of soil and water, destruction of biodiversity, and the spread of toxic pollution from pesticides and chemical fertilizers'.[27] Shiva's words echo those written by Marx 150 years ago, which stated,

> All progress in capitalist agriculture ... is a progress in the art, not only of robbing the worker, but of robbing the soil; all progress in increasing the fertility of the soil for a given time is a progress towards ruining the more long-lasting sources of that fertility. ... Capitalist production, therefore, only develops the techniques and the degree of combination of the social process of production by

simultaneously undermining the original sources of all wealth – the soil and the worker.[28]

Communities around the world are responding to these issues in creative and inspiring ways. Indigenous peoples in Latin America have fought to defend their own vision of nature and development not only through the actions of popular movements in the region but also by enshrining the 'rights of Mother Earth' into law in countries such as Bolivia and Ecuador. The principles and values of what is known as *Buen Vivir*, the Good Life, have provided the pillars for this movement. *Buen Vivir* refers to an alternative view of development that captures the 'Good Life' in the broadest sense of the term. It emerged in the late 1990s, partly as a critique of the austerity programs implemented by the IMF and the World Bank, but also as a critique of Western development strategies, which had debatable results both in terms of the environment and in terms of who benefits economically. Not surprisingly, the movement grew up in tandem with the recent rise of socialist movements and governments in the region led by Venezuela's late-president Hugo Chávez, Ecuador's President Rafael Correa and Bolivia's President Evo Morales.

Eduardo Gudynas explains that while the *Buen Vivir* approach has its variants across communities and cultures, 'It includes the classical ideas of quality of life, but with the specific idea that well-being is only possible *in community* (my emphasis). Furthermore in most approaches, the community concept is understood in the expanded sense, to include

Nature'.[29] The current capitalist development model continues to emphasize the types of development that colonialism was built upon, and *Buen Vivir* provides a language that challenges this approach. As Gudynas explains, 'Such radical questioning was possible within several indigenous traditions in South America, which culturally lacked concepts like development or progress. The contribution of indigenous knowledge to Buen Vivir therefore continues to be a critical thread.'[30]

So while large-scale, externally-oriented, authoritarian projects and programs dominate the development agenda of the major international institutions and the foreign policy of most global North states, the lack of sustainability – on all fronts from environmental to democratic – of this model is becoming ever more visible. In Bolivia this contradiction is particularly glaring given that the economy is dependent on the extractive industry with 70 per cent of exports derived from minerals and natural gas. The government of President Evo Morales, which self-identifies as both indigenous and socialist, has depended on this revenue to tackle poverty and to support industrialization. As journalist Federico Fuentes points out, 'A central challenge facing progressive governments and social movements in South America today is breaking the region's dependency on raw material exports. This issue, which has tended to revolve around the concept of "extractivism", has also become one of the main points of contention between supporters and critics of the processes of change currently underway in the region'.[31] Many of the movements that have emerged have self-identified as socialist and in the emphasis placed on the rights of nature and collective responsibility for the land, reflect broader notions of interdependence.

But the contradictions evident in Bolivia have led some analysts to doubt the power of the new law that enshrines the rights of Mother Earth to seriously challenge the extractivist model there. As Jim Schultz of the Cochabamba-based Democracy Center notes, 'If Mother Earth truly did have legal standing then the indigenous peoples protesting the government's plan to construct a highway through the rainforest would certainly be able to use it to challenge that highway. In the end, the pretty words of the law, sadly, have little impact on the ambitious mining and other environmentally destructive activities being carried out across the country'.[32] Therefore, until these types of changes reflect a genuine shift to democracy in the sphere of production and in the broader economy, they have the danger of remaining largely symbolic.

Clearly, the kinds of changes needed to build genuine democracies extend beyond the contemporary legal frame-works and may often actually challenge current laws. However, the inclusion of the rights of Mother Earth in the constitution of Ecuador (2008) and the legal framework of Bolivia (2009) can be seen as important steps forward in terms of the formal codification of these rights and the potential legitimization of a new paradigm that these rights imply. It is one way of recognizing in law the notion of interdependence. Gudynas notes that the approach in each country has been quite different. In Bolivia, *Buen Vivir* goes to the heart of the values of the state itself. In Ecuador, the emphasis is more on laying out a set of rights, many of which can be found in the Western tradition (freedom, participation, protection, etc.) with the innovation being the extension of these rights to nature. Speaking of Bolivia, Catherine Walsh explains,

> In a country that has long exalted its *mestizo* character, favoured whitening and whiteness, and looked to the North for its model of development, the incorporation of buen vivir as the guiding principle of the Constitution is historically significant. Its new conceptualization as public policy is a result largely of the social, political, and epistemic agency of the indigenous movement over the last two decades. It responds to the urgency of a radically different social contract that presents alternatives to capitalism and the 'culture of death' of its neo-liberal and development project.[33]

The concept of Mother Earth, as now entrenched in Bolivian law, is based on a broad definition rooted in multicultural indigenous concepts including 'harmonious living', 'the good life', 'land without evil' and 'the noble life'.[34] It is a vision of nature that includes humans and other animals; it is about the interconnectedness of the entire web of life. This web of life is defined as:

> complex and dynamic communities of plants, animals, micro-organisms and other beings in their environment, in which human communities and the rest of nature

interact as a functional unit, under the influence of climatic, physiographic and geologic factors, as well as the productive practices and cultural diversity of Bolivians of both genders, and the world views of Indigenous nations and peoples, intercultural communities and the Afro-Bolivians.[35]

The law, which echoes Buddhist notions of interdependence, defines Mother Earth as 'a collective subject of public interest' and as 'the dynamic living system formed by the indivisible community of all life systems and living beings whom are interrelated, interdependent, and complementary, which share a common destiny'.[36] Clearly, the potential implications of the law for building a more compassionate democracy and interconnected citizenship are vast. The law constitutes an example of the institutionalization of the Dalai Lama's idea of universal responsibility and, if enforced, could challenge the basis of the capitalist development model. The socialist policies implemented in Bolivia have already reduced the poverty and inequality inherent in the neoliberal model. Under Morales, poverty has been reduced by 25 per cent and extreme poverty by 50 per cent. Between 2005 and 2012 the minimum wage increased by 87.7 per cent and the healthcare budget more than tripled. Furthermore, infant and maternal mortality rates have decreased significantly. In tandem with these impressive social achievements, Bolivia's economy has an average annual growth rate of 5.1 per cent and boasts the second lowest inflation rate in South America.[37]

In Ecuador, *Buen Vivir* is expressed in the indigenous Quechua concept of *sumak kawsay*, which refers to 'a fullness in life in a community, together with other persons and nature'.[38] Gudynas argues that the Ecuadorian version may ultimately be more powerful than its Bolivian counterpart because it openly declares that the development model of the state must be in line with *Buen Vivir* in order to fulfil the rights of Mother Earth, or *Pachamama*. These rights include nature's right to regeneration and restoration, the use of precaution and restriction mechanisms to protect species from extinction, and the rights of individuals and groups to appear before public bodies to defend these rights. Also, significantly, the Constitution states, 'Nature is subject to those rights given by this Constitution and Law.'[39]

By acknowledging the rights of nature and entrenching them in the legal frameworks of the state, Bolivia and Ecuador have created the possibility of turning the capitalist model of development inside-out by presupposing the inter-connectedness of all living things and a new citizenship based upon interdependence. As Schilling-Vacaflor notes, this new 'constitutionalism' that includes nature rights is evidence of 'the intent to overcome the deficiencies of previous democratic models, which were characterized by a wide gap between the state and civil society, high levels of social inequality, and deficient recognition of cultural diversity'.[40]

But it is important to recognize that these legal changes are taking place in the context of an epochal shift to the Left in Latin American politics over the past couple of decades with leaders in Bolivia, Ecuador and Venezuela identifying as socialists. After a clear citizen endorsement of his socialist policies in his 2009 electoral victory, Ecuadorian President Rafael Correa declared,

> We have formal democracy, our great challenge now is to build true democracy, which means a more fair and more equal homeland ... Socialism will continue. The Ecuadorian people voted for that. We are going to emphasize this fight for social justice, for regional justice. We are going to continue the fight to eliminate all forms of workplace exploitation within our socialist conviction: the supremacy of human work over capital. Nobody is in any doubt that our preferential option is for the poorest people, we are here because of them. *Hasta la victoria siempre!* (Until victory, forever)'.[41]

In this vein, the attempts to entrench the rights of nature into the legal system in countries such as Ecuador and Bolivia should be seen as part of a broader movement to build big C compassion into the economy and political process. In countries across the region there has been an attempt to transform the old way of doing politics in Latin America which, like in all so-called 'capitalist democracies' in the global South, has disproportionately favoured elites. And the outcomes across the region, particularly in states identifying as socialist, have been impressive in this regard.

Even *The Economist* magazine reluctantly acknowledged the 'skill' of President Correa in achieving impressive economic results in Ecuador considering an inherited dependence on foreign remittances and oil exports and the impacts of the 2008 global financial crisis and subsequent world recession. Poverty in Ecuador has been reduced by 27 per cent since 2006 and in 2013 unemployment reached its lowest level in 25 years. Meanwhile, social spending has increased significantly particularly in education and healthcare.[42] Despite these social gains, some on the left have criticized Correa because the contradictions that exist in Bolivia between the concept of *Buen Vivir* and extractivism are also visible in Ecuador. It is the country's oil revenues that have funded the social gains, particularly in urban areas. Meanwhile, many indigenous groups continue to be negatively impacted by the government's extractivist policies.[43]

While such contradictions need to be addressed, they don't change the fact that one would be hard pressed to find a capitalist global South country that has even come close to Bolivia and Ecuador with regard to reducing poverty, dramatically improving access and delivery of healthcare, significantly reducing rates of infant and maternal mortality and improving democratic participation of the citizenry at all levels of governance.

All of the alternative perspectives discussed above – from Earth Democracy to eco-socialism – emphasize the idea of inclusion and the maintenance of democratic decision-making power as close to the community level as possible. In effect, we are talking about the expression of compassion in political processes and the implementation of genuine democracy, which is never conceived of as separate from economic activity.

Communities in the global North and South continue to grapple with the reality of trying to survive economically in the global capitalist system as they construct alternatives while simultaneously resolving their own internal contradictions around issues of race, gender, other species and nature. Meanwhile, the Transition Town movement, the New Economy Movement, the Tiny House movement, and community gardens and farmers' markets are just some examples of the growing consciousness in the global North around consumerism and our impact on nature. According to sociologist Tracey Harris,

> As more people question the status quo with respect to housing and consumption, it necessarily draws into question societal values. As momentum is gained, it draws into criticism the culture of overconsumption, consumerism, and environmental degradation. Building community and status separate from demonstrations of economic prowess and consumptive clout begins to shift the kind of societal values we share and can lead to cultural adaptations.[44]

Throughout this book I have explored the interlinked oppressions evident in the exploitation of humans, other animals and nature, pointing to the need for a structural perspective that makes visible the lines of accountability in order to move towards a more compassionate world. We have seen in this chapter how there are various alternative perspectives and approaches emerging that recognize the ways in which we are alienated from other humans, non-human animals and nature. All of these approaches recognize in their own ways the centrality of the idea of interdependence and with this the necessity of embodying this idea in our daily practices, which includes everything from new approaches to our food to the kinds of work we engage in. These approaches all emphasize the land – and variously all living things – along with its importance to culture and the necessity of democratic control at the local level.

Embedded in this vision is a view of the interdependence of people and nature, and while non-human animals are not always mentioned explicitly, it embodies a compassionate vision of protecting species diversity and integrity – plant and animal – and suggests that any strict division of species used to justify exploitation is both ethically problematic and unsustainable. Drawing on the Star Trek approach which, although fictional, nicely expresses the attitude of a compassionate society, Sue Donaldson and Will Kymlicka explain, 'The USS Enterprise encounters many species incapable of producing Shakespeare (or Spock or Data), human language, or human moral reflection, and yet all are approached with the same ethic of respect for their own uniquely adaptive intelligence and consciousness'.[45]

The goal here has been to highlight the need to shift our political and economic culture so that it emphasizes the respectful and ethical treatment of humans, other animals and nature in order to establish the basis for a compassionate democracy. If such ethical principles were to guide our interactions with humans and other animals in all pursuits it would create a significant shift in global equality, democracy and citizenship. Almost all countries and communities are currently caught up in the logic of capitalism, which promotes conventional, large-scale development and agriculture as essential for putting food on the table while simultaneously fuelling a seemingly insatiable consumer appetite. But there is a paradox in this approach because the very model that is presented as necessary to ensure our survival also threatens our survival.

Challenging the capitalist model is not an easy sell, particularly in the global North, because it means that we have to re-evaluate our worldview and change our lifestyles, or, as Buddhists would say cultivate the 'right view' and challenge our habitual patterns by consuming less, and engaging compassionately with the people and other animals that are impacted by our daily practices. For socialists, this radical shift in values requires a fundamental shift in our political and economic institutions, a shift that democratizes the economy, recognizes the value of labour and celebrates the uniqueness and potential of all human beings. For both Buddhists and socialists, we need to begin the move towards this model in the here and now, in our current roles and communities, and among all the challenges of where we find ourselves today. Building a new compassionate ethic rooted in interconnected citizenship requires that we see ourselves and our future as inextricably connected to the health and wellbeing of all humans, other animals and nature.

CONCLUSION

Love for others and respect for their rights and dignity, no matter who or what they are: ultimately these are all we need. So long as we practice these in our daily lives, then no matter if we are learned or unlearned, whether we believe in Buddha or God, or follow some other religion or none at all, as long as we have compassion for others and conduct ourselves with restraint out of a sense of responsibility, there is no doubt we will be happy. — The Dalai Lama

If we have chosen the position in life in which we can most of all work for mankind, no burdens can bow us down, because they are sacrifices for the benefit of all; then we shall experience no petty, limited, selfish joy, but our happiness will belong to millions, our deeds will live on quietly but perpetually at work, and over our ashes will be shed the hot tears of noble people. — Karl Marx

I was outside trudging through the late December snow to take Christmas decorations down to the basement and began thinking about how quickly things change. On the cold stone steps just inside the door, I caught sight of a furry little caterpillar all curled up but still alive. I was in a rush to get back upstairs to the kids, so I left him there. But upstairs back in the warm I reflected on what I should do about the caterpillar. Was he better off on the basement stairs just inside the door? Or should I try to find him a warmer place where he could eat and drink? Where would that be? Did he need to eat and drink? Or was he about to build a cocoon that would keep him safe and warm until that day when he would emerge as a beautiful butterfly? Then I laughed at myself. What do I know about caterpillars? Not much. I do know that I care about them and hope that no one steps on them. And I'm very curious about how they transform themselves from one thing into another. I have also heard that caterpillars struggle to get out of their cocoons but that it is actually not a good idea to help them at that stage of their development because they are building strength for what lies ahead.

Sitting down at my computer, I realized that these were the types of thoughts and feelings I was having when I came to write this conclusion. Many of us become quite skilled at explaining what is wrong with ourselves, our lives and with the world in general, but when it comes to figuring out what to do about it and then actually doing it, we often get stumped. Do I do this or that? What would really be helpful? Everything we do could in some way cause harm or good – like mowing the lawn pleases the neighbour while killing millions of insects. Or constructing a wind turbine reduces greenhouse gas emissions but may also imperil already vulnerable migratory bird species.

As we have seen, the Buddhist way of thinking about interdependence recognizes that all of our behaviours and practices have effects, some of which we are not even aware. And when it comes to human beings, we can't really be entirely mathematical or scientific in our analysis given that human behaviour is not robotic. As much as mainstream economists and others try to put us in measureable boxes, we are unpredictable, emotional and constantly changing. And thank goodness for that! For Buddhists, the point is that we try not to intentionally cause harm. And socially-engaged Buddhists would emphasize that we think collectively and socially about this approach to life. In other words, when we know we can make another choice that does not cause harm, or is at least less harmful, then we should make the commitment to do that. If we add a Marxist framework to this, we would ensure that our measurement of harm does not just look at isolated individual behaviours but looks also at structural and institutional harms.

Drawing on what I think are some essential kernels of wisdom in the Marxist and Buddhist traditions, I have argued in these pages that when we begin to glimpse the reality of our interdependence with all living things, we also begin to see the world with more compassionate eyes and learn not only to better understand the 'other', but to really appreciate them. This leads us to ask why there is so much suffering in the world and what we can do about it, and how can we find ways to celebrate our diversity and difference rather than punish each other for them.

I have tried to show how harm and violence are both individual and structural problems. At an individual level we need to give up on our delusion of separateness from other beings and nature. It is this delusion that leads to the greed, hatred and violence of our world. We have seen how the history of capitalism has depended upon genocide, slavery and the destruction of nature, and that our contemporary economic system continues to rely on violence and exploitation in the forms of neo-colonialism, ongoing imperialism and consumerism. As the bodies in the basement pile up, we in the global North in particular and increasingly the wealthier classes in the global South, need to recognize that rampant consumerism itself is a form of structural violence. Our lifestyles continue to be dependent on systems of production and consumption that are built on alienation and exploitation and, ultimately, on violence both physical and structural.

The gift that Marx gave the world is a way of seeing that allows us to understand how this violence and suffering exists in social and economic institutions that often appear benign. He also showed that throughout history economic elites have disproportionately benefited from the political and economic arrangements of the day. And to ensure their privilege, elites have also controlled the dominant messages of society through education and media to the degree that the general population comes to see the values of the ruling class as their own values by existing in a state of false consciousness. Finally, in providing a critique of the commodification of all life, Marx gave us tools to understand the roots of much of our personal alienation in capitalist culture. He showed that average everyday people create value for society every time they work and yet they have little control over the fruits of their labour or the wealth it creates.

A Marxist perspective allows us to see how the economic structures of our society embody particular forms of alienation that lead to violence and suffering and that whether or not we take action we are contributing to the future. Therefore, Marxists and Buddhists suggest that rather than living on auto pilot, we could more intentionally work to create the future we want. In this, it becomes clear that what we do in the realm of our day-to-day lives as parents, teachers, plumbers or musicians is incredibly important. But Marxists remind us that a structural approach is also essential. It will be difficult to bear the fruits of all our good work at an individual level if the capitalist system remains in place. While paying close attention to our individual behaviours, we should simultaneously work more intentionally towards creating institutional structures that reflect big C compassion, a compassion that has no hierarchy and no borders.

Recognizing our interdependence, and effectively turning compassion into a verb, requires that we get the 'right view' of the situation both from a historical perspective, looking back with a compassionate and empathetic reading of history, and by gaining a clear view of our current circumstances. This would allow us to do what our indigenous brothers and sisters have historically asked of us, to take the long view of time by thinking beyond the current generation and recognizing the contributions and mistakes of our ancestors and by thinking about how our behaviours impact future generations. This requires that we re-evaluate our definitions of progress and success and that we reclaim our education and media systems and demand that they serve our needs as globally interdependent and diverse peoples rather than serving the dictates of elites and the needs of capital. When we give up our delusion of separateness and challenge the elite control of our systems of socialization, a whole bunch of exciting possibilities arise for a more socially just world. But, as I have argued, this requires that we work for a radical democratization of our societies and the global system beginning right where we find ourselves today at home, at work and in the community.

Baseball legend Yogi Berra once said, *'The future ain't what it used to be'*. And this is how I feel whenever I think about the structural and institutional harms that have led us to our current global situation and that threaten our survival. On issues like climate change it just feels like the future is much closer than it used to be and there is a sense of real urgency to act now for a more compassionate world. Among other things, that means working daily on ourselves, in our homes, in our workplaces and in our communities to think about more compassionate ways of being and doing. A key part of that job is confronting all the forms of alienation that we experience under capitalism: from ourselves, from each other, from non-human animals and from nature.

However, I don't believe we can change ourselves or others by simply imposing ecological or ethical accountability upon ourselves and others. In fact, our ego attachments ensure that attempts to do so can often backfire, with people becoming defensive and digging their heels in. It is like trying to demand that someone in their heart be non-homophobic. We can make laws and protect people against homophobia but we may still find that some people obeying the laws harbour those feelings. This speaks to what the Dalai Lama calls 'our overall state of heart and mind', and each of us has our own journey in this regard.[1] As individuals we will have to work on ourselves in order to, as Buddhists would say, get to know our own minds and hearts. If we get into the habit of thinking more intentionally about the harm and suffering in all that we do, we will inevitably strengthen particular values, such as recognizing that others feel pain and insecurity just as we do and that we actually share – in the kindergarten sandbox-type of way – a planet. As previously noted, the problem is that even if we don't *do* anything, if we live on auto pilot, we are still reinforcing a specific set of values, but they might not be the ones that we want to reinforce. This is true both on an individual level (habitual patterns and addictions) and on a societal level (social attitudes and behaviours). In this sense, and as Marxists remind us, the status quo is already political and ideological.

Marx said that 'philosophers have hitherto only interpreted the world in various ways; the point is to change it'.[2] It is clear that societies express values through their laws, institutions and social practices and there is what Marx would call a 'dialectical' (constantly interacting and influencing) relationship between institutional reinforcement and individual change. For this reason we need to confront head on the 'problem of production', realizing that how we make decisions around the way we organize our economy is a fundamental part of any meaningful democracy. For some of us this implies that the end of our system of capitalism, while not the entire solution, is a necessary prerequisite for creating a just and ecologically viable future. There is no simple magic bullet that will get us there but that shouldn't stop us from saying it's necessary. Individual communities will have to decide for themselves, democratically, how they want to move forward and there will be approaches that are culturally appropriate to specific contexts.

It is clear that in the early twenty-first century there is a growing recognition of interdependence and the need for more compassionate political and economic systems in various communities, social movements and projects around the world. People are organizing in new and creative ways to build self-reliance and genuine democracy: from the New Economy Movement and Transition Towns to the landless workers' movement in Brazil; from the cooperative movement in Argentina to independent indigenous media cooperatives in Colombia; from Navdanya and Earth Democracy in India to community gardens in Detroit; and from cooperative housing in the Netherlands to Tiny living in California. Additionally, broad-based expressions of discontent with the way things are have been expressed in the anti-globalization movement and in movements such as Occupy and Idle No More and in the international campaigns against global free trade and austerity programmes. All of these movements are expressions of a desire to gain control over our everyday lives and to live more meaningfully in community and in solidarity with people everywhere, irrespective of race or religion, and in harmony with the Earth.

While Marx sought to open the world's eyes to the injustices inherent in the capitalist system, his ultimate goal was to help us realize that we can overcome them. And Buddhism similarly seeks to let us know how we can live free from suffering. Buddhism complements Marxism's orientation towards positive social change by showing how our individual alienation is rooted in our misunderstanding about the nature of being. Believing that we are separate from other people, non-human animals and nature leads us to try to protect what we believe to be ours against 'others'. In contrast, understanding our own minds and hearts will lead us to the eternal and universal truth that is not specific to any religion or belief system and that is actually reinforced by science: our interdependence. For all of these reasons, it becomes obvious why someone with the experience and wisdom of the Dalai Lama would declare himself a Buddhist Marxist.

I have argued here that a clear understanding of our interdependence leads us to act more compassionately in the world. And the more we act this way – both individually and collectively – the more others will feel empowered to begin pulling out arrows and to initiate the transition to a more compassionate and sustainable global society rooted in the recognition of our interdependence. Achieving such a revolutionary transformation might seem like a formidable challenge. But as Nelson Mandela once reminded us, 'It always seems impossible until it's done'.

NOTES

Introduction

1 Ruchi Kumar, 'I'm a Socialist and a Marxist, Says the Dalai Lama During His Mumbai Visit', *Daily News and Analysis*, 31 May 2014.

2 Patrice Ladwig and Mark Shields, 'Introduction to Special Issue: Against Harmony? Radical and Revolutionary Buddhism(s) in Thought and Practice', *Politics, Religion and Ideology*, 15(2), 2014, pp.187–204.

3 Oxfam International, *An Economy for the 1%: How Privilege and Power in the Economy Drive Extreme Inequality and How this Can Be Stopped*, Oxfam International Briefing Paper 210, 2016, p.2.

4 Oxfam Great Britain, *Even It Up: Time to End Extreme Inequality* (Cowley: Oxfam Great Britain, 2014).

5 Stephanie Nebehay, 'World's Refugees and Displaced Exceed Record 60 Million: U.N.', Reuters, 18 December 2015.

6 If you are new to Marx, you may be interested in reading Rius's playful *Marx for Beginners* (New York: Pantheon Books, 2003) or Peter Singer's *Marx: A Very Short Introduction* (Oxford: Oxford Paperbacks, 2000). And, if you're terrified just reading the first page of *Capital*, check out the new edition of David Smith's *Marx's Capital Illustrated* (Chicago: Haymarket Books, 2014).

7 Terry Eagleton, *Why Marx Was Right* (New Haven: Yale University Press, 2011), p.3.

8 Sakyong Mipham Rinpoche is the leader of the International Shambhala Movement and he argues that our view of human nature is intimately connected to our capacity to change our world for the better.

9 While there is an overwhelming literature to explore on Buddhist social theory, I would like to recommend any and all books by Zen

teacher and social activist David L. Loy. For a very contemporary Buddhist take on everything from poverty and punishment to technology and war, see Loy's *The Great Awakening: A Buddhist Social Theory* (Somerville: Wisdom Publications, 2003).

10   For very practical and constructive ways to deal with the pain of our world, I would recommend any and all of Macy's work, and I will return to her ideas later on, but for now you may be interested in her most recent book co-authored with Chris Johnstone, *Active Hope: How to Face the Mess We're In Without Going Crazy* (Novato: New World Library, 2012).

11   Stuart Smithers, 'The Spiritual Crisis of Capitalism: What Would the Buddha Do?', *Adbusters*, 29 June 2012.

1. Much ado about no-thing

1   Albert Einstein from a letter to Robert S. Marcus on the occasion of his son passing away. Letter accessed online at *The Liberator Magazine*, 21 December 2015.

2   See Thomas McFarlane (ed.), *Einstein and Buddha: The Parallel Sayings* (Berkeley: Ulysses Press, 2002) and Matthieu Ricard and Trinh Xuan Thuan, *The Quantum and the Lotus* (New York: Three Rivers Press, 2001) for a more detailed discussion on the parallels between quantum interdependence and Buddhist interdependence.

3   According to *The Times Literary Supplement* (1995), Ernst Friedrich 'Fritz' Schumacher's *Small is Beautiful: A Study of Economics as if People Mattered* (1973) is among the 100 most influential books published since World War II.

4   Sulak Sivaraksa, *The Wisdom of Sustainability: Buddhist Economics for the 21st Century* (Kihei: Ko Books, 2009), p. 31.

5   Karl Marx, *Economic and Philosophical Manuscripts of 1844* (Amherst, NY: Prometheus Books, 1988), p. 20.

6   Noam Chomsky, *On Power and Ideology* (New York: Black Rose Books, 1987), p. 27.

7   Terry Jones (director), *Monty Python's Life of Brian*, Cinema International Corporation, 1979.

8   Robert E. Lane, 'Friendship or Commodities? The Road Not Taken: Friendship, Consumerism and Happiness', in Neva R. Goodwin, Frank Ackerman and David Kiron (eds), *The Consumer Society* (Washington: Island Press, 1997), p. 104.

9   Richard Layard, 'Happiness: Has Social Science a Clue?', London School of Economics, Lionel Robbins Memorial Lectures, March 2003.

10 James Reveley, 'Understanding Social Media Use as Alienation: A Review and Critique', *E-Learning and Digital Media*, 10(1), February 2013, pp. 83–94.

11 Mike Davis, *Planet of Slums* (London: Verso, 2006), p. 176.

12 Slavoj Žižek, *First as Tragedy, Then as Farce* (London: Verso, 2009), p. 103.

13 Karl Marx, *The Poverty of Philosophy* (Moscow: Progress Publishers, 1955).

14 Barbara Noske, *Beyond Boundaries: Humans and Animals* (Montreal: Black Rose Books, 1997), p. 13.

15 Ibid., pp. 18–21.

16 David Nibert, *Animal Rights/Human Rights: Entanglements of Oppression and Liberation* (Latham, MD: Rowman and Littlefield Publishers, 2002), p. 214.

17 Ibid.

18 Vic Bishop, 'The Illusion of Choice: Ninety Per Cent of American Media Controlled by Six Corporations', Centre for Research on Globalization, 29 August 2015.

19 Robert W. McChesney, *Corporate Media and the Threat to Democracy* (New York: Seven Stories Press, 1997).

20 Robert W. McChesney, 'Global Media, Neoliberalism, and Imperialism', *Monthly Review*, March 2001.

21 Sophie Fiennes (director), *The Pervert's Guide to Ideology*, Zeitgeist Films, 2012.

2. Compassion is a verb

1   While derived from teachers in the Tibetan Buddhist lineage, the Shambhala teachings form the groundwork for a largely

secular movement that since the time of its founder Chögyam Trungpa Rinpoche has provided teachings and trainings mostly to Westerners. See Chögyam Trungpa, *The Sacred Path of the Warrior* (Boston: Shambhala Publications, 1984) for a wonderful treatise on the cultivation of bravery.

2   Mipham J. Mukpo, *The Shambhala Principle: Discovering Humanity's Hidden Treasure* (New York: Random House, 2013), pp. 17–18.

3   Trungpa, *The Sacred Path of the Warrior*, p. 8.

4   Ibid., p. 9.

5   If you are interested in further explanation of the Buddhist approach to cultivating these characteristics, see Pema Chödrön, *The Wisdom of No Escape: And the Path to Loving Kindness* (Boston: Shambhala Publications, 2001) and Alan Wallace, *The Four Immeasurables: Practices to Open the Heart* (Boston: Shambhala Publications, 2010).

6   Trungpa, *The Sacred Path of the Warrior*, p. 10.

7   Ethan Nichtern, *One City: A Declaration of Interdependence* (Somerville: Wisdom Publications, 2007), p. 166.

8   In no way do I mean to suggest that individual soldiers from our Western nations are not brave people. Rather I am suggesting that many of the wars that our countries are currently engaged in are driven by misguided principles and are not ultimately making any of us safer. I am pointing to an alternative approach to bravery at an individual and institutional level that would make war redundant.

9   Terry Gibbs and Tracey Harris, 'Compassionate Democracy: Citizenship and the Living World', *Global Social Justice Journal*, 2(1), October 2015. Also, see the various works of David Nibert for an analysis of the life of food animals under capitalism both historically and in contemporary times. Additionally, the documentary film *Cowspiracy* details the environmental impacts of factory farming. And to gain an understanding of the specific issues involved in lobbying for animal rights see the websites of

Mercy for Animals, Compassion in World Farming, and People for the Ethical Treatment of Animals.

10 See the documentary *Speciesism: The Movie* (2013) directed by Mark Devries for a provocative often humorous look at how humans see themselves in relation to non-human animals.

11 See Melanie Joy, *Why We Love Dogs, Eat Pigs and Wear Cows* (San Francisco: Conari Press, 2010) for an engaging analysis of our contradictory attitudes towards animals.

12 Margaret Wente, 'The Charitable and the Cheap: Which One Are You?' *Globe and Mail* online, 20 January 2007.

13 Kimberly J. Morgan, 'America's Misguided Approach to Social Welfare', *Foreign Affairs*, January/February 2013.

14 Ibid.

15 Elizabeth Rosenthal, 'What Makes Europe Greener than the U.S.?' *Yale Environment 360*, 28 September 2009.

16 Ibid.

17 For an excellent overview of global inequalities and differences between the global North and global South see, Oxfam Great Britain, *Even It Up: Time to End Extreme Inequality* (Cowley: Oxfam Great Britain, 2014) and the more recent Oxfam International Briefing Paper *An Economy for the 1%: How Privilege and Power in the Economy Drive Extreme Inequality and How this Can Be Stopped.*

18 Dalai Lama, 'Universal Responsibility in the Modern World', Public Talk, Royal Albert Hall, London, 22 May 2008. Transcript accessed from the website of His Holiness the 14th Dalai Lama of Tibet, December 2015.

19 For Buddhists this understanding comes through 'practice'. When someone becomes a Buddhist they are said to 'take refuge' in the 'three jewels', that is the Buddha, the Dharma and the Sangha. Depending on the text/interpretation, the 'Buddha' can refer to the historical person, Siddhārtha Gautama who became enlightened, or the idea of the enlightened potential that exists within all beings or both; the Dharma (in Sanskrit) or Dhamma

(in Pali, the language of the oldest Buddhist texts) refers to the Buddha's teachings and sometimes the nature of 'truth' or 'reality' itself, and the Sangha, while sometimes referring to those who have attained enlightenment and may help others to do so or to the community of Buddhist monks and nuns, more popularly refers to the broader community of practicing Buddhists.

20 See Chapter 13 in Pema Chödrön, *Comfortable with Uncertainty* (Boston: Shambhala Publications, 2003) for a very accessible explanation of the four noble truths.

21 Pema Chödrön, *Living Beautifully with Uncertainty and Change* (Boston: Shambhala Publications, 2012), p. 7.

22 Lama Surya Das, *Awakening the Buddha Within* (New York: Broadway Books, 1997), p. 83.

23 Ibid.

24 There are many great books explaining the Noble Eightfold Path. I have found works by Theravada Buddhist monk Bikkhu Bodhi to be very accessible. See in particular, Bhikkhu Bodhi, *The Noble Eightfold Path: The Way to the End of Suffering* (Kandy: Buddhist Publication Society, 1998).

25 Walpola Rahula, *What the Buddha Taught* (New York: Grove Press, 1974), p. 49.

26 I have found these two books particularly helpful: Pema Chödrön's *How to Meditate: A Practical Guide to Making Friends with Your Mind* (Boston: Sounds True, 2013) and the Sakyong Mipham's *Ruling Your World: Ancient Strategies for Modern Life* (New York: Doubleday Broadway Publishing 2005).

27 David Loy, 'The Karma of the Rings' in Jonathan S. Watts (ed.) *Rethinking Karma: The Dharma of Social Justice.* (Bangkok: International Network of Engaged Buddhists, 2014), p. 239.

28 David Loy, 'What's Buddhist about Socially Engaged Buddhism?' *Un Zen Occidental*, February/March 2004.

3. Living in an alienated world

1   See Robert E. Buswell Jr. and Donald S. Lopez Jr., '10 Misconceptions about Buddhism: #5, Buddhism is a Philosophy and Not a Religion', Tricycle Blog Series: 10 Misconceptions about Buddhism, 29 May 2014, for the argument for Buddhism as religion.

2   The Tripitaka is the canon of both Theravada and Mahayana Buddhists and can be found in languages such as Pali, Chinese and Tibetan. Tripitaka (Tipitaka in Pali) refers to texts whose authorship is attributed directly or indirectly to the Buddha.

3   Terry Eagleton, *Why Marx was Right* (New Haven: Yale University Press, 2011), pp. 66–67.

4   Garry Leech, *Capitalism: A Structural Genocide* (London: Zed Books, 2012), p. 11.

5   Johan Galtung, J., 'Violence, Peace and Peace Research', *Journal of Peace Research*, 6(3), 1969, p. 171.

6   Leech, *Capitalism*, p. 149.

7   See ibid.

8   See Joel Kovel, *The Enemy of Nature: The End of Capitalism or the End of the World?* (London: Zed Books, 2007).

9   Ivan Mészáros. I. *The Structural Crisis of Capital* (New York: Monthly Review Press, 2010), p. 144.

10 UNICEF, 'The State of the World's Children 2005: Childhood Under Threat', United Nations, December 2004.

11 Deepa Bhatia (director), *Nero's Guests*, Mistral Movies, 2009.

12 In actuality, for those considering reincarnation as a cow, the next life might not be as luxurious as the Indian farmer suggests. While cows may indeed be getting stuffed with ample quantities of grain, this does not speak to whether this is ultimately good for the health and wellbeing of the cows or us, or whether it is good for the environment. Cows are often crammed into Confined Animal Feeding Operations (CAFOs) that are responsible for massive pollution. Additionally, in order to ensure the speed and efficiency of the animals' growth and to deal with the fact that

cow stomachs are not naturally made to eat grain, the industry is dependent on the massive use of growth hormones and antibiotics which in turn is leading to the spread of antibiotic-resistance bacteria and increased prevalence of pathogenic E-coli (found, for example, in undercooked hamburgers). See 'The Truth About Grassfed Beef' (2012) and other related resources on the website of *The Food Revolution Network* guided by John and Ocean Robbins.

13 Ellen Meiksins Wood in Larry Patriquin (ed.), *The Ellen Meiksins Wood Reader* (Leiden: Brill Academic Publishing, 2012), p. 297.

14 Garry Leech, 'Revolution in the United States', *Counterpunch*, 7 November 2014.

15 Ellen Meiksins Wood in Patriquin (ed.), *The Ellen Meiksins Wood Reader*, p. 298.

16 Leech, *Capitalism*, pp. 32–33.

17 See the International Labour Organization website, ilo.org, Forced Labour, Human Trafficking and Slavery section (accessed 10 December 2015) and the US Department of State, *Trafficking in Persons Report* (Washington DC: Department of State, 2015).

18 Chris Hedges, *Empire of Illusion: The End of Literacy and Triumph of Spectacle* (New York: Nation Books, 2009), p. 103.

19 Nicolaus Mills, 'The Corporatization of Higher Education', *Dissent Magazine* online, Fall 2012.

20 Taiaiake Alfred, 'First Nations Perspectives on Political Identity', *First Nation Citizenship Research and Policy Series: Building Towards Change*, Assembly of First Nations, June 2009, pp. 2–3.

21 Tamsin McMahon, 'Why Fixing First Nations Education Remains So Far Out of Reach', *Macleans* online, 22 August 2014.

22 Ngugi wa Thiong'o, *Decolonising the Mind: The Politics of Language in African Literature* (Portsmouth: Heinemann, 1986), p.3. See also, Waziyatawin and Michael Yellow Bird, *For Indigenous Minds Only: A Decolonization Handbook* (Santa Fe: School for Advanced Research Press, 2012).

23 See Derrick Jensen et al., *Unsettling Ourselves: Reflections and Resources for Deconstructing the Colonial Mentality* (Unsettling Minnesota Collective, 2009) for an excellent sourcebook on what decolonization may entail for settlers.

24 Donald Grinde and Bruce Johansen, *Exemplar of Liberty: Native America and the Evolution of Democracy* (Los Angeles: Amer Indian Studies Center, 1991) and Bruce Johansen, *Forgotten Founders: How the American Indian Helped Shape Democracy* (Boston: Harvard Common Press, 1982).

25 Bruce Johansen, *Forgotten Founders: How the American Indian Helped Shape Democracy* (Boston: Harvard Common Press, 1982).

26 Samuel Bowles and Herbert Gintis. *Schooling in Capitalist America: Educational Reform and the Contradictions of Economic Life* (Chicago: Haymarket Books, 2011)

27 Sumitra, 'Japan's Okinawa Island: The Healthiest Place on Earth', *Oddity Central* online, 26 March 2012.

4. Consumer citizens in a globalized society

1 Jeanna Bryner, 'The Power of Advertising', *Live Science*, 9 March 2010.

2 Eric Chivian and Aaron Bernstein (eds), *Sustaining Life: How Human Health Depends on Biodiversity* (New York: Oxford University Press, 2008).

3 E. F. Schumacher, *Small is Beautiful: Economics as if People Mattered* (Vancouver: Hartley and Marks Publishers, 1999), p. 248.

4 In a fascinating discussion on the long view of time, Joanna Macy and Chris Johnstone calculate the history of the earth represented as a single day. They show how the entire history of the human species is represented in the last five seconds before midnight. Macy and Johnstone, *Active Hope: How to Face the Mess We're In Without Going Crazy* (Novato: New World Library, 2012), p. 153.

5   Garry Leech, 'The Elephant in the Room: Capitalism and Sustainable Development', *Counterpunch*, 15 October 2015.

6   To pursue this in further detail, an excellent starting point is the special issue of the journal *Politics, Religion and Ideology* (2014), No. 2, Against Harmony? Radical and Revolutionary Buddhism(s) in Thought and Practice, which discusses this complex history and points to further reading. Also see Noam Chomsky, 'The Soviet Union Versus Socialism', *Our Generation*, Spring/Summer 1986.

7   Mipham J. Mukpo, *The Shambhala Principle: Discovering Humanity's Hidden Treasure* (New York: Random House, 2013), p. 20.

8   Ibid.

9   It is also true that Christianity has a long tradition of self-reflection and immanent critique. One can find many parallels to Eastern religions evident in the non-mainstream teachings such as the Gnostic Gospels, in writings of the mystics such as Thomas Merton and in movements such as Liberation Theology.

10 Read all his books! See in particular Mipham J. Mukpo, *Ruling Your World: Ancient Strategies for Modern Life* (New York: Doubleday Broadway Publishing, 2005) and Mukpo, *The Shambhala Principle*.

11 Mukpo, *The Shambhala Principle*, p. 20.

12 While there are volumes written about this, recent interesting and rigorous analyses on this theme include Naomi Klein, *This Changes Everything* (Toronto: Vintage Canada, 2014); Garry Leech, *Capitalism: A Structural Genocide* (London: Zed Books, 2013) and Thomas Piketty, *Capital in the Twenty-First Century* (Boston: Harvard University Press, 2014).

13 George McRobie quoted in the video 'Small is Working: Technology for Poverty Reduction', UNESCO, Intermediate Technology Development Group and Television Trust for the Environment, 2004.

14 Schumacher, *Small is Beautiful*, p. 4.

15 Ibid., p. 1.

16 See David Nibert, *Animal Rights/Human Rights: Entanglements of Oppression and Liberation* (Latham, MD: Rowman and Littlefield Publishers, 2002) for a Marxist take on the intersections of human and non-human animal oppression.

17 Andrew J. Bacevich, 'He Told Us to Go Shopping. Now the Bill is Due', *Washington Post* online, 5 October 2008.

18 Ibid.

19 Ibid.

20 President Barack Obama, 'Remarks by the President to the 113th National Convention of the Veterans of Foreign Wars', VFW Convention Hall, Reno, Nevada, 23 July 2012, The Whitehouse, Office of the Press Secretary.

21 For an excellent analysis of the corporatization of the media, see Robert McChesney, *Corporate Media and the Threat to Democracy* (New York: Seven Stories Press, 1997).

22 Franco 'Bifo' Berardi, *Heroes: Mass Murder and Suicide* (London: Verso Books, 2015).

23 Catherine O'Brien, 'Sustainability, Happiness and Education', *Journal of Sustainability Education*, Vol. 1, May 2010, p. 1.

24 Sulak Sivaraksa, *The Wisdom of Sustainability: Buddhist Economics for the 21st Century* (Kihei: Ko Books, 2009), p. 90.

25 Norberg-Hodge is the founder and director of the International Society for Ecology and Culture (ISEC). See www.localfutures. org.

26 Helena Norberg-Hodge, *Ancient Futures: Learning From Ladakh* (London: Rider, 1991).

27 Helena Norberg-Hodge, *Ancient Futures: Lessons from Ladakh for a Globalizing World* (San Francisco: Sierra Club Books, 2009), p. 204.

28 Helena Norberg-Hodge, Steven Gorelick and John Page (directors), *The Economics of Happiness*, International Society for Ecology and Culture, 2011.

29 Helena Norberg-Hodge, 'The Economics of Happiness', *Countercurrents.org*, 26 February 2010.

30 Helena Norberg-Hodge, 'Compassion in the Age of the Global Economy', in Gay Watson, Stephen Batchelor and Guy Claxton (eds), *The Psychology of Awakening* (New York: Random House, 2000).

31 Norberg-Hodge, 'The Economics of Happiness'.

32 Leech, *Capitalism*, p. 40.

33 'Living Planet Report 2006', World Wildlife Fund, 2006, p. 19.

34 Pope Francis, *Apostoltic Exhortation on the Proclamation of the Gospel in Today's World*. The Vatican, 24 November 2013, note 56.

35 Ibid., note 59.

36 Ibid.

37 Ed Stourton, 'Is the Pope a Communist', *BBC News Magazine* online, June 2015.

38 Karl Marx, *Capital: Volume 1: A Critique of Political Economy* (London: Penguin, 1992), p. 799.

39 See Piketty, *Capital in the Twenty-first Century*.

40 See Leech, *Capitalism*.

41 See Klein, *This Changes Everything*.

42 Karl Marx, *Economic and Philosophic Manuscripts of 1844* (Amherst, NY: Prometheus Books, 1988), p. 76.

5. Bodies in the basement

1 Truth and Reconciliation Commission of Canada, *Honouring the Truth: Reconciling for the Future*, 2015.

2 Tamsin McMahon, 'Why Fixing First Nations Education Remains So Far Out of Reach', *Macleans Magazine* Online, 22 August 2014.

3 Ibid.

4 Edward Goldsmith, 'Development as Colonialism' in Jerry Mander and Edward Goldsmith (eds), *The Case Against the*

Global Economy: And for a Turn Towards Localization (London: Earthscan, 2000), p. 20.

5   See Steven Swinford and Christopher Hope, 'Children Should be Taught about Suffering Under the British Empire, Jeremy Corbyn Says', *The Telegraph* online, 27 July 2015, and Jonathan Jones, 'The Tories' Corbyn Attack Video is Absurd, Paranoid and Nasty – And Will Work', *The Guardian* online, 14 September 2015.

6   See Taiaiake Alfred, *Peace, Power, Righteousness: An Indigenous Manifesto* (Oxford: Oxford University Press, 1999), Samir Amin, *Global History: A View from the South* (Oxford: Pambazuka Press, 2011), Franz Fanon, *The Wretched of the Earth* (New York: Grove Press, 1963), Eduardo Galeano, *Open Veins of Latin America* (New York: Monthly Review Press, 1997) and Edward Said, *Orientalism* (New York: Random House, 1979).

7   Galeano, *Open Veins of Latin America*, p. 2.

8   See Robert J. Miller, Jacinta Ruru, Larissa Behrendt and Tracey Lindberg, *Discovering Indigenous Lands: The Doctrine of Discovery in the English Colonies* (Oxford: Oxford University Press, 2012) for a rigorous analysis by indigenous scholars of the implications of this doctrine.

9   Ibid.

10   Said, *Orientalism*, p. xix.

11   Jeffrey Sachs, *The End of Poverty* (New York: Penguin Books, 2005).

12   Vandana Shiva, 'New Emperors, Old Clothes', *The Ecologist*, published online 1 July 2005.

13   See Traleg Kyabgon Rinpoche, *Karma: What It Is, What It Isn't and Why It Matters* (Boston: Shambhala Publications, 2015) for a rigorous analysis of this much misunderstood concept.

14   David Nibert, *Animal Oppression and Human Violence: Domesecration, Capitalism and Global Conflict* (New York: Columbia University Press, 2013), p. 268.

15 Joanna Macy and Chris Johnstone, *Active Hope: How to Face the Mess We're in Without Going Crazy* (Novato: New World Library, 2012), p. 15.

16 Antonio Gramsci, *Selections from the Prison Notebooks* (New York: International Publishers: 1971).

17 The act of silencing dissent has been formalized in many US states with 'ag-gag' laws. In a 2011 *New York Times* column Mark Bittman coined the term 'ag-gag' to refer to state laws that forbid the act of undercover filming or photography of activity on farms without the consent of their owner. The main targets of these laws are of course the whistleblowers who uncover animal rights abuses. The sad reality in capitalist democracies is that most citizens do not have Oprah's millions to fight back.

18 The couple's story is told in the film *McLibel: The Postman and Gardener Who Took on McDonald's and Won*, directed by Franny Armstrong and Ken Loach (1997, re-released 2005)

19 Marjorie Olster, 'GMO Foods: Key Points in the Genetically Modified Debate', *Huff Post Green* online, 8 February 2013.

20 Sarah Boseley, 'Sugar Industry Threatens to Scupper WHO', *The Guardian* online, 21 April 2003.

21 Francie Diep, 'How Sugar Lobbying Influenced US Government-Funded Research', *Pacific Standard* online, 10 March 2015.

22 Paul Battersby, Joseph M. Siracusa and Sasho Ripiloski, *Crime Wars: The Global Intersection of Crime, Political Violence, and International Law* (Santa Barbara, CA: Praeger, 2011), p. 139.

23 Inez Benitez, 'Two Children May Have Died for You to Have Your Mobile Phone', Interpress Service News Agency, 12 September 2012.

24 Sheng Yun, 'Accidental Death of a Poet', *London Review of Books* online, 11 November 2014.

25 For a more detailed analysis of this and other cases see Franicso Ramírez, *The Profits of Extermination: How U.S. Corporate Power is Destroying Colombia* (Monroe: Common Courage Press, 2005) and Terry Gibbs and Garry Leech, *The Failure of Global*

Capitalism: From Cape Breton to Colombia and Beyond (Sydney: Cape Breton University Press, 2009).

26 Garry Leech, 'The Elephant in the Room: Capitalism and Sustainable Development', *Counterpunch*, 15 October 2015.

27 Helena Norberg-Hodge, *Ancient Futures: Learning From Ladakh* (London: Rider, 1991).

28 It should be noted that obesity has a variety of causes, eating a diet high in calories is just one of them. People who are overweight do not necessarily eat more than the rest of us. Other factors include environment, family genes, lack of sleep, certain medications such as anti-depressants, and health conditions. Here I am referring to the obesity caused by high calorie diets and the lack of access to decent nutrition.

29 Excellent research and discussion on the effects of the Western diet on health are available in documentary films such as *Food Inc.* (2008), *Forks Over Knives* (2011) and *Fed Up* (2014). Also see *The Food Revolution Network* website for further resources and online courses.

30 Data taken from Kip Anderson and Keegan Kuhn (producers), *Cowspiracy: The Sustainability Secret*, First Spark Media, 2015.

31 Jeff Anhang and Robert Goodland, *Livestock and Climate Change* (Worldwatch.org, 2009), p. 13.

32 Henning Steinfeld, Pierre Gerber, T. D. Wassenaar, Vincent Castel, Mauricio Rosales and Cees de Haan, *Livestock's Long Shadow: Environmental Issues and Options* (Food and Agriculture Organization of the United Nations, 2006).

33 Ibid.

34 United States Environmental Protection Agency, 'Overview of Greenhouse Gases', http://epa.gov, accessed 4 December 2015.

35 Gene Bauer with Gene Stone, *Living the Farm Sanctuary Life: The Ultimate Guide to Eating Mindfully, Living Longer, and Feeling Better Every Day* (New York: Rodale, 2015).

6. Capitalism and the democratic deficit

1   Dalai Lama, *How to Practice: The Way to a Meaningful Life* (New York: Atria Books, 2002), p. 80.

2   Carmen DeNavas-Walt and Bernadette D. Proctor, *Income and Poverty in the United States: 2014*, United States Census Bureau, US Department of Commerce, September 2014.

3   Dan Levy, 'Banking on Airports: Q&A with HSBC's Global Advertising Head', *Sparksheet*, 29 January 2010.

4   Joseph Stiglitz, 'On the Wrong Side of Globalization', *New York Times* online, 15 March 2014.

5   Ibid.

6   Ibid.

7   Garry Leech, *Capitalism: A Structural Genocide* (London: Zed Books, 2012), p. 40.

8   Joel Kovel, *The Enemy of Nature: The End of Capitalism or the End of the World?* (London: Zed Books, 2007), p. 123.

9   See Chris Paine (director), *Who Killed the Electric Car?*, Electric Entertainment, 2006.

10   See Theresa Tedesco, 'The Uneasy Ties Between Canada's Universities and Wealthy Business Magnates', *Financial Post* online, 9 March 2012 and Joel Westheimer, 'Higher Education or Education for Hire?: Corporatization and the Threat to Democratic Thinking', *Academic Matters*, Ontario Confederation of University Faculty Associations, April–May 2010 for reflections on this theme.

11   Tedesco, 'The Uneasy Ties'.

12   'Ayn Rand – Playboy Interview', *Playboy Magazine*, March 1964.

13   In fact Meiksins Wood argues that world peace is impossible under capitalism. See Ellen Meiksins Wood, *Democracy Against Capitalism: Renewing Historical Materialism* (New York: Cambridge University Press, 1995).

14   Grahame Russell, 'The Pathological Inter-Connection Between Bombing, Investing and Caring', *Rights Action*, 27 November 2015.

15   Francis Fukuyama, *The End of History and the Last Man* (New York: Avon Books, 1992).

16   For an example of Albert Einstein's socialist views, see 'Why Socialism?', *Monthly Review*, 1(1), May 1949.

17   Oxfam Great Britain, *Even It Up: Time to End Extreme Inequality* (Cowley: Oxfam Great Britain, 2014).

18   Kathrin Brandmeir et al., *Allianz Global Wealth Report 2015* (Munich: Allianz, 2015).

19   'Capitalism and Its Critics: A Modern Marx', *The Economist* online, 3 May 2014.

20   Ibid.

21   See the work of the late Charles Bowden and Dawn Paley for excellent on the ground analyses of the impact of 'free trade' on the average Mexican.

7. In search of the global citizen

1   On 10 September 1813, after defeating the British fleet in the Battle of Lake Erie during the War of 1812, US Navy Commodore Oliver Hazard Perry dispatched this now infamous message to Major General William Henry Harrison: 'Dear Gen'l: We have met the enemy, and they are ours, two ships, two brigs, one schooner and one sloop. Yours with great respect and esteem. H. Perry.' Walt Kelly paraphrased the statement in his cartoon strip *Pogo* and used it on the poster he designed for the observance of the first Earth Day on 22 April 1970.

2   Mipham J. Mukpo, *The Shambhala Principle: Discovering Humanity's Hidden Treasure* (New York: Random House, 2013), pp. 42–43.

3   Ernesto 'Che' Guevara, 'Socialism and Man in Cuba', in D. Deutschmann (ed.), *Che Guevara Reader: Writings on Politics and Revolution* (Melbourne: Ocean Press, 2003).

4   Moh Hardin, *A Little Book of Love: Heart Advice on Bringing Happiness to Ourselves and Our World* (Boston: Shambhala Publications, 2011), pp. 79–80.

5   Bill Martin, 'Bring on the Crack-Up: Hoping for a Trump-Sanders Election', *Counterpunch*, 26 March 2016.

6   See the most recent report of climate scientists James Hansen et al., 'Ice Melt, Sea Level Rise and Superstorms: evidence from paleoclimate data, climate modeling, and modern observations that 2° C global warming could be dangerous', *Atmos. Chem. Phys.*, 16, 2016, pp. 3761–3812. The report suggests that things are much worse than we think and that dealing with the problem is not about slowing the growth of emissions but requires that we stop them entirely.

7   Dalai Lama, *My Tibet* (London: Thames and Hudson, 1990), pp. 79–80.

8   David Held, 'Restructuring Global Governance: Cosmopolitanism, Democracy and the Global Order', *Millennium-Journal of International Studies*, 37(3), 2009, p. 454.

9   Richard Bellamy, *Citizenship: A Very Short Introduction* (Oxford: Oxford University Press, 2008), p. 71.

10 Val Plumwood, 'Shadow Places and the Politics of Dwelling', *Australian Humanities Review*, Issue 44, 2008, p. 142.

11 See the Democracy Ranking Association, democracyranking.org.

12 Karl Marx, *Capital: Volume 1: A Critique of Political Economy* (London: Penguin, 1992), p. 876.

13 Joel Kovel, *The Enemy of Nature: The End of Capitalism or the End of the World?* (London: Zed Books, 2007), p. 271.

14 Ibid., p. 151.

15 David Nibert, *Animal Rights/Human Rights: Entanglements of Oppression and Liberation* (Latham, MD: Rowman and Littlefield Publishers, 2002), p. 247.

16 Kovel, *The Enemy of Nature*, p. 272.

17 See Naomi Klein, *This Changes Everything: Capitalism vs. the Climate* (Toronto: Vintage Canada, 2014) for countless examples.

18 Email from Canadian eco-socialist Ian Angus, 2 January 2013.

19 Ibid., p.2.

20 Vandana Shiva, *Earth Democracy: Justice, Sustainability and Peace* (Cambridge, MA: South End Press, 2005), p. 9.

21 Ibid., p. 5.

22 Ibid., pp. 9–11.

23 While this may not satisfy those working for animal rights or veganism, it is clearly a massive step in the right direction. The Navdanya Biodiversity Farm itself, the actual site of the 'Earth University' only serves vegetarian food.

24 Ibid., p. 149.

25 See Navdanya, navdanya.org, accessed 23 October 2015.

26 See Navdanya, navdanya.org, accessed 23 October 2015.

27 Shiva, *Earth Democracy*, p. 151.

28 Marx, *Capital, Volume 1*, p. 638.

29 Eduardo Gudynas, 'Buen Vivir: Today's Tomorrow', *Development*, 54(4), 2011, p. 441.

30 Ibid., p. 442.

31 Frederico Fuentes, 'Bolivia and the Large Scale Extraction of Natural Resources: Beyond (neo)extractivism?', Centre for Research on Globalization, 19 August 2014.

32 Emily Achtenberg, 'Earth First? Bolivia's Mother Earth Law Meets the Neo-Extractivist Economy', *NACLA: Rebel Current*, 16 November 2012.

33 Catherine Walsh, 'Development as Buen Vivir: Institutional Arrangements and (de) Colonial Entanglements', *Development*, 53(1), 2010, p. 18.

34 Gudynas, 'Buen Vivir', p. 3.

35 Asamblea Legislativa Plurinacional de Bolivia 2010, *Ley de Derechos*, Articulo 4.

36 Ibid., Articulos 3 y 4.

37 W. T. Whitney, 'Clouds Gather Over Bolivia's Change Process as US Intervenes', *Counterpunch*, 16 February 2016.

38 Gudynas, 'Buen Vivir', p.3.

39 Asamblea Constituyente, Republica del Ecuador, *Constitución de la Republica,* 2008.

40 Almut Schilling-Vacaflor, 'Bolivia's New Constitution: Towards Participatory Democracy and Political Pluralism?', *European Review of Latin American and Caribbean Studies*, 90, 2011, p.16.

41 Enrico Tortolano, 'Revolution on March as Correa Makes History', *Tribune Magazine*, 30 April 2009.

42 Marc Weisbrot, 'Why Ecuador Loves Rafael Correa', *The Guardian*, 15 February 2015.

43 Paul Gottinger, 'Correa and Ecuador's Left: An Interview with Marc Becker', *Upside Down World*, 1 June 2016.

44 Tracey Harris, 'Living Tiny: A Richer and More Sustainable Future', *Counterpunch*, 15 July 2015.

45 Sue Donaldson and Will Kymlicka, *Zoopolis: A Political Theory of Animal Rights* (Oxford: Oxford University Press, 2011), p. 257.

Conclusion

1   His Holiness the Dalai Lama, *Ethics for the New Millennium* (New York: Riverhead Books, 1999), p. 32.

2   Karl Marx, 'Theses on Feuerbach', Marxists.org, 1845.

BIBLIOGRAPHY

Achtenberg, E. (2012) 'Earth First? Bolivia's Mother Earth Law Meets the Neo-Extractivist Economy.' *NACLA: Rebel Current*, 16 November.

Adams, C. (1994) *Neither Man nor Beast: Feminism and the Defense of Animals*. New York: Continuum.

Alfred, T. (2009) 'First Nations Perspectives on Political Identity.' *First Nation Citizenship Research and Policy Series: Building Towards Change*, Assembly of First Nations, June.

Alfred, T. (1999) *Peace, Power, Righteousness: An Indigenous Manifesto*. Oxford: Oxford University Press.

Amin, S. (2011) *Global History: A View from the South*. Oxford: Pambazuka Press.

Andersen, K. and K. Kuhn (producers). (2015) *Cowspiracy: The Sustainability Secret*. First Spark Media.

Anhang J. and Robert Goodland. (2009) *Livestock and Climate Change*. Worldwatch.org.

Armstrong, F. and K. Loach (directors). (1997, 2005) *McLibel: The Postman and Gardener Who Took on McDonald's and Won*. London: Spanner Films.

Asamblea Constituyente, Republica del Ecuador. (2008) *Constitución de la Republica del Ecuador*.

Asamblea Legislativa Plurinacional de Bolivia. (2010) *Ley de Derechos de Madre Tierra, Ley 071*, 21 December.

Ashcroft, B., Gareth Griffiths and Helen Tiffin. (2013) *Post-Colonial Studies: The Key Concepts*, Third Edition. New York: Routledge.

Bacevich, A. (2008) 'He Told Us to Go Shopping. Now the Bill is Due.' *Washington Post* online, 5 October.

Barlow, M. (2015) *Blue Future: Protecting Water for People and the Planet Forever.* Toronto: House Anansi Press.

Batchelor, S. (2015) *After Buddhism.* New Haven: Yale University Press.

Bauer, G. with G. Stone. (2015) *Living the Farm Sanctuary Life: The Ultimate Guide to Eating Mindfully, Living Longer, and Feeling Better Every Day.* New York: Rodale.

Bellamy, R. (2008) *Citizenship: A Very Short Introduction.* Oxford: Oxford University Press.

Bhikkhu, T. (2011) 'Selves & Not-self: The Buddhist Teaching on Anatta: Talk One.' Access to Insight. Online.

Bishop, V. (2015) 'The Illusion of Choice: Ninety Per Cent of American Media Controlled by Six Corporations.' Centre for Research on Globalization, 29 August.

Bodhi, B. (1998) *The Noble Eightfold Path: The Way to the End of Suffering.* Kandy: Buddhist Publication Society.

Boseley, S. (2003) 'Sugar Industry Threatens to Scupper WHO.' *The Guardian* online, 21 April.

Bowles, S. and Herbert Gintis. (2011) *Schooling in Capitalist America: Educational Reform and the Contradictions of Economic Life.* Chicago: Haymarket Books.

Brandmeir, K., M. Grimm, M. Heise and A. Hozhausen. (2015) *Allianz Global Wealth Report 2015.* Munich: Allianz.

Chödrön, P. (2013) *How to Meditate: A Practical Guide to Making Friends with Your Mind.* Boston: Sounds True.

Chödrön, P. (2012) *Living Beautifully with Uncertainty and Change.* Boston: Shambhala Publications.

Chödrön, P. (2003) *Comfortable with Uncertainty.* Boston: Shambhala Publications.

Chödrön, P. (2001) *The Wisdom of No Escape: And the Path to Loving Kindness.* Boston: Shambhala Publications.

Chomsky, A., G. Leech and S. Striffler (eds) (2007) *The People Behind Colombian Coal: Mining, Multinationals and Human Rights.* Bogotá: Casa Editorial Pisando Callos.

Chomsky, N. (1986) 'The Soviet Union Versus Socialism.' *Our Generation*, Spring/Summer.

Dalai Lama. (2009) 'Universal Responsibility and the Climate Emergency', in Stanley, J., David R. Loy and Gyurme Dorje (eds). *A Buddhist Response to the Climate Emergency*. Somerville: Wisdom Publications.

Dalai Lama. (1999) *Ethics for the New Millennium*. New York: Riverhead Books.

Dalai Lama. (1990) *My Tibet*. London: Thames and Hudson.

Davis, M. (2006) *Planet of Slums*. London: Verso.

Dellorto, D. (2012) 'Global Report: Obesity Bigger Health Crisis than Hunger.' *CNN Online*.

DeNavas-Walt, C. and Bernadette D. Proctor. (2014) 'Income and Poverty in the United States: 2014.' United States Census Bureau, US Department of Commerce, September.

Devries, M. (director). (2013) *Speciesism: The Movie*. Mark Devries Productions.

Donaldson, S. and W. Kymlicka. (2011) *Zoopolis: A Political Theory of Animal Rights*. Oxford: Oxford University Press.

Dumasy, T. (2015) '3 Reasons Why Supporting Peace is More Important Than Ever.' *Devex: International Development News*, 18 December.

Eagleton, T. (2011) *Why Marx was Right*. New Haven: Yale University Press.

Economist. (2014) 'Capitalism and Its Critics: A Modern Marx.' *The Economist* online, 3 May.

Einstein, A. (1950) accessed from *The Liberator Magazine*, 21 December 2015.

Fanon, F. (2005) *The Wretched of the Earth*. New York: Grove Press.

Flynn, C. P. (2004) 'Gender, Power, and Control: A Sociologist Looks at the Link between Animal Abuse and Family Violence.' Keynote paper presented at *Linking Violence: An Interdisciplinary Conference on the Relationship between Violence Against Animals* and Humans, University College of Cape Breton, Sydney, Nova Scotia.

Francis, Pope. (2013) Apostolic Exhortation on the Proclamation of the Gospel in Today's World. The Vatican, 24 November.

Fuentes, F. (2014) 'Bolivia and the Large Scale Extraction of Natural Resources: Beyond (neo)extractivism?' Centre for Research on Globalization, 19 August.

Fukuyama, F. (1992) The End of History and the Last Man. New York: Avon Books.

Galeano, E. (1997) Open Veins of Latin America. New York: Monthly Review Press.

Galtung, J. (1969) 'Violence, Peace and Peace Research.' Journal of Peace Research, 6(3).

Garcia, C. and G. Gutiérrez (directors). (2009) The Coca-Cola Case: The Truth that Refreshes. Argus Films and National Film Board of Canada.

Gibbs, T. and G. Leech (2009) The Failure of Global Capitalism: From Cape Breton to Colombia and Beyond. Sydney: Cape Breton University Press.

Gibbs, T. and T. Harris. (2015) 'Compassionate Democracy: Citizenship and the Living World.' Global Social Justice Journal, 2(1), October.

Gimenez, M. E. (2001) 'Marxism, and Class, Gender, and Race: Rethinking the Trilogy.' Race, Gender and Class, 8(2), Special Issue on Marxism, pp. 23–33.

Goodland, R. and J. Anhang. (2009) Livestock and Climate Change. WorldWatch.

Gramsci, A. (1971) Selections from the Prison Notebooks. New York: International Publishers.

Greene, N. (n.d.) 'The First Successful Case of the Rights of Nature Implementation in Ecuador.' Global Alliance for the Rights of Nature, accessed 29 March 2016.

Greenwood, M., S. de Leeuw, N. M. Lindsay and C. Reading (eds). (2015) Determinants of Indigenous Peoples' Health in Canada: Beyond the Social. Toronto: Canadian Scholars' Press.

Grinde, D. and Johansen, B. (1991) *Exemplar of Liberty: Native America and the Evolution of Democracy*. Los Angeles: Amer Indian Studies Center.

Gudynas, E. (2011) 'Buen Vivir: Today's Tomorrow.' *Development*, 54(4): 441–447.

Hardin, M. (2011) *A Little Book of Love*. Boston: Shambhala Publications.

Harris, T. (2015) 'Living Tiny: A Richer and More Sustainable Future.' *Counterpunch*, 15 July.

Hedges, C. (2010) *Empire of Illusion: The End of Literacy and Triumph of Spectacle*. Toronto: Vintage Canada.

Held, D. (2009) 'Restructuring Global Governance: Cosmopolitanism, Democracy and the Global Order.' *Millennium-Journal of International Studies*, 37(3): 535–547.

Hope Alkon, A. and J. Agyeman (eds). (2011) *Cultivating Food Justice: Race, Class and Sustainabilty*. Boston: MIT Press.

International Institute for Strategic Studies. (2015) *Armed Conflict Survey 2015*. London: International Institute for Strategic Studies.

Jensen, D. et al. (2009) *Unsettling Ourselves: Reflections and Resources for Deconstructing the Colonial Mentality*. Unsettling Minnesota Collective.

Johansen, B. (1982) *Forgotten Founders: How the American Indian Helped Shape Democracy*. Boston: Harvard Common Press.

Jones, J. (2014) 'The Tories' Corbyn attack video is absurd, paranoid and nasty – and will work.' *The Guardian* online, 14 September.

Joy, M. (2010) *Why We Love Dogs, Eat Pigs, and Wear Cows: An Introduction to Carnism*. San Francisco: Conari Press.

Kaufman, D. and P. C. Vicente. (2005) 'Legal Corruption.' *Munich Personal RePEc Archive*, MPR Paper 8186, posted 10 April 2008.

Kaul, I., P. Conceicão, K. Le Goulven and R. Mendoza (eds). (2003) *Providing Global Public Goods*. Oxford: Oxford University Press.

Klein, N. (2014) *This Changes Everything*. Toronto: Vintage Canada.

Kovel, J. (2007) *The Enemy of Nature: The End of Capitalism or the End of the World?* London: Zed Books.

Kyabgon, T. (2015) *Karma: What It Is, What It Isn't and Why It Matters*. Boston: Shambhala Publications.

Lane, R. (1997) 'Friendship or Commodities? The Road Not Taken: Friendship, Consumerism and Happiness', in N. Goodwin, Frank Ackerman and David Kiron (eds) *The Consumer Society*. Washington: Island Press.

Layard, R. (2003) 'Happiness: Has Social Science a Clue?' London School of Economics: Lionel Robbins Memorial Lectures, March.

Leech, G. (2016) *How I Became an American Socialist*. South Bar: Misfit Books.

Leech, G. (2015) 'The Elephant in the Room: Capitalism and Sustainable Development.' *Counterpunch*, 15 October.

Leech, G. (2012) *Capitalism: A Structural Genocide*. London: Zed Books.

Lingam, L. (2005) 'Structural Adjustment, Gender and Household Survival Strategies: Review of Evidences and Concerns.' Center for the Education of Women, University of Michigan.

Loy, D. (2015) *A New Buddhist Path: Enlightenment, Evolution and Ethics in the Modern World*. Somerville: Wisdom Publications.

Loy, D. (2014) 'The Karma of the Rings' in Jonathan S. Watts (ed.) *Rethinking Karma: The Dharma of Social Justice*. Bangkok: International Network of Engaged Buddhists.

Loy, D. (2008) *Money, Sex, War, Karma: Notes for a Buddhist Revolution*. Somerville: Wisdom Publications.

Loy, D. (2004) 'What's Buddhist about Socially Engaged Buddhism?' Paris: Un Zen Occidental.

Loy, D. (2003) *The Great Awakening: A Buddhist Social Theory*. Somerville: Wisdom Publications.

Lundin, D. (2015) 'Malnutrition in America.' *Livestrong.com*, 28 July.

Macy, J. and C. Johnstone. (2012) *Active Hope: How to Face the Mess We're in without Going Crazy*. Novato: New World Library.

Martin, B. (2016) 'Bring on the Crack-Up: Hoping for a Trump-Sanders Election.' *Counterpunch*, 26 March.

Marx, K. (1992) *Capital: A Critique of Political Economy, Volume 1.* London: Penguin.

Marx, K. (1984) *Economic and Philosophical Manuscripts of 1844.* New York: Prometheus Books.

McChesney, R. (2001) 'Global Media for Global Control.' *Third World Traveller: Educate Magazine*, October to December.

McChesney, R. (1997) *Corporate Media and the Threat to Democracy.* New York: Seven Stories Press.

McFarlane, T. (ed.) (2002) *Einstein and Buddha: The Parallel Sayings.* Berkeley: Ulysses Press.

McMahon, T. (2014) 'Why Fixing First Nations Education Remains So Far Out of Reach.' *Macleans*, 22 August.

Mészáros. I. (2010) *The Structural Crisis of Capital.* New York: Monthly Review Press.

Miller, R. J., J. Ruru, L. Behrendt and T. Lindberg (2012) *Discovering Indigenous Lands: The Doctrine of Discovery in the English Colonies.* Oxford: Oxford University Press.

Mills, N. (2012) 'The Corporatization of Higher Education.' *Dissent Magazine* online, Fall 2012.

Morgan, K. J. (2013) 'America's Misguided Approach to Social Welfare.' *Foreign Affairs Online, Essay*, January/February Issue.

Morrow, R. A. and C. A. Torres. (1995) *Social Theory and Education.* Albany: SUNY Press.

Mukpo, M. J. (2013) *The Shambhala Principle: Discovering Humanity's Hidden Treasure.* New York: Random House.

Mukpo, M. J. (2005) *Ruling Your World: Ancient Strategies for Modern Life.* New York: Doubleday.

National Council of Welfare (2012) 'Poverty Profile, Special Edition: A Snapshot of Racialized Poverty in Canada.' Government of Canada.

Ngugi wa Thiong'o. (1986) *Decolonising the Mind: The Politics of Language in African Literature.* Portsmouth: Heinemann.

Nibert, D. (2013) *Animal Oppression and Human Violence: Domesecration, Capitalism, and Global Conflict.* New York: Columbia University Press.

Nibert, D. (2002) *Animal Rights/Human Rights: Entanglements of Oppression and Liberation.* Latham, MD: Rowman and Littlefield Publishers.

Nichtern, E. (2007) *One City: A Declaration of Interdependence.* Somerville: Wisdom Publications.

Norberg-Hodge, H. (2009) *Ancient Futures: Lessons from Ladakh for a Globalizing World.* San Francisco: Sierra Club Books.

Norberg-Hodge, H. (2000) 'Compassion in the Age of the Global Economy', in Gay Watson, Stephen Batchelor and Guy Claxton (eds), *The Psychology of Awakening.* New York: Random House.

Norberg-Hodge, H. (1991) *Ancient Futures: Learning From Ladakh.* London: Rider.

Noske, B. (1997) *Beyond Boundaries: Humans and Animals.* Montreal: Black Rose Books.

Nussbaum, M. (2012) *Why Democracy Needs the Humanities.* Princeton: Princeton University Press.

Obama, B. (2012) 'Remarks by the President to the 113th National Convention of the Veterans of Foreign Wars.' VFW Convention Hall, Reno, Nevada, 23 July. Accessed from United States Government, The Whitehouse, Office of the Press Secretary, 10 December 2015.

O'Brien, C. (2010) 'Sustainability, Happiness and Education.' *Journal of Sustainability Education*, May, Vol. 1, p.1.

Olster, M. (2013) 'GMO Foods: Key Points in the Genetically Modified Debate.' *Huff Post Green* online, 8 February.

Oxfam Great Britain. (2014) *Even It Up: Time to End Extreme Inequality.* Cowley: Oxfam Great Britain.

Oxfam International. (2016) *An Economy for the 1%: How Privilege and Power in the Economy Drive Extreme Inequality and How this Can Be Stopped.* Oxfam International Briefing Paper 210.

Paine, C. (director). *Who Killed the Electric Car?* Electric Entertainment, 2006.

Palmer, G. (n.d.) 'Low Income and Ethnicity'. *The Poverty Site*, accessed 2 December 2014.

Piketty, T. (2014) *Capital in the Twenty-first Century.* Boston: Harvard University Press.

Plumwood, V. (2008) 'Shadow Places and the Politics of Dwelling.' *Australian Humanities Review*, Issue 44, pp.139–150.

Rahula, W. (1974) *What the Buddha Taught.* New York: Grove Press.

Ramirez, F. (2005) *The Profits of Extermination: How U.S. Corporate Power is Destroying Colombia.* Monroe: Common Courage Press.

Reveley, J. (2013) 'Understanding Social Media Use as Alienation: A Review and Critique.' *E-Learning and Digital Media*, 10(1): 83–94.

Ricard, M. and Trinh Xuan Thuan. (2001) *The Quantum and the Lotus.* New York: Three Rivers Press.

Rius. (2003) *Marx for Beginners.* New York: Pantheon Books.

Rosenthal, E. (2009) 'What Makes Europe Greener than the U.S.?' *Yale Environment 360*, 28 September.

Ryder, R. (1989) *Animal Revolution: Changing Attitudes Towards Speciesism.* Oxford: Basil Blackwell.

Sachs, J. (2005) *The End of Poverty.* New York: Penguin Books.

Said, E. (1979) *Orientalism.* Vintage Books Edition. New York: Random House.

Schilling-Vacaflor, A. (2011) 'Bolivia's New Constitution: Towards Participatory Democracy and Political Pluralism?' *European Review of Latin American and Caribbean Studies*, 90: 3–22.

Schumacher, E. F. (1999) *Small is Beautiful: Economics as if People Mattered.* Vancouver: Hartley and Marks Publishers.

Shiva, V. (2013) *Making Peace with the Earth*. London: Pluto Press.

Shiva, V. (2005) *Earth Democracy: Justice, Sustainability and Peace*. Cambridge, MA: South End Press.

Shiva, V. (2005) 'New Emperors, Old Clothes.' *The Ecologist*, 1 July.

Shiva, V. (2002) *Water Wars: Privatization, Pollution and Profit*. Toronto: Between the Lines.

Shiva, V. (1989) *Staying Alive: Women, Ecology and Development*. London: Zed Books.

Singer, P. (2000) *Marx: A Very Short Introduction*. Oxford: Oxford Paperbacks.

Singer, P. and J. Mason. (2006) *The Ethics of What We Eat: Why Our Food Choices Matter*. Emmaus, PA: Rodale.

Sivaraksa, S. (2009) *The Wisdom of Sustainability: Buddhist Economics for the 21st Century*. Kihei: Ko Books.

Smith, D. and P. Evans (2014) *Marx's Capital Illustrated*. Chicago: Haymarket Books.

Soechtig, S. (director). (2014) *Fed Up*. Atlas Films.

Stanley, J., D. R. Loy and G. Dorje (eds). (2009) *A Buddhist Response to the Climate Emergency*. Somerville: Wisdom Publications.

Steckley, J. and G. K. Letts. (2013) *Elements of Sociology: A Critical Canadian Introduction*, third edition. Don Mills, ON: Oxford University Press.

Steinfeld, H., P. Gerber, T. D. Wassenaar, V. Castel, M. Rosales and C. de Haan. (2006) *Livestock's Long Shadow: Environmental Issues and Options*. Food and Agriculture Organization of the United Nations.

Stiglitz, J. (2014) 'On the Wrong Side of Globalization.' *New York Times* online, 15 March.

Sumitra. (2012) 'Japan's Okinawa Island: The Healthiest Place on Earth.' *Oddity Central* online, 26 March.

Surya Das, Lama. (1997) *Awakening the Buddha Within*. New York: Broadway Books.

Swinford, S. and C. Hope. (2015) 'Children Should Be Taught about Suffering under the British Empire, Jeremy Corbyn Says.' *The Telegraph* online, 27 July.

Tedesco, T. (2012) 'The Uneasy Ties Between Canada's Universities and Wealthy Business Magnates.' *Financial Post* online, 9 March.

Thich Nhat Hanh. (2013) *Love Letter to the Earth*. Berkeley: Parallax Press.

Thich Nhat Hanh. (2005) *Being Peace*. Berkeley: Parallax Press.

Tortolano, E. (2009) 'Revolution on March as Correa Makes History.' *Tribune Magazine*, April 30.

Trungpa, C. (2009) *Smile at Fear: Awakening the True Heart of Bravery*. Boston: Shambhala Publications.

Trungpa, C. (1984) *The Sacred Path of the Warrior*. Boston: Shambhala Publications.

UNESCO. (2004) 'Small is Working: Technology for Poverty Reduction'. UNESCO, Intermediate Technology Development Group and Television Trust for the Environment.

US Department of State. (2015) *Trafficking in Persons Report*. Washington, DC: Department of State.

US Environmental Protection Agency. (n.d.) 'Overview of Greenhouse Gases', accessed 4 December 2015.

Vaughan-Lee, L. (ed.) (2014) *Spiritual Ecology: The Cry of the Earth*. Point Reyes: The Golden Sufi Center.

Wallace, A. (2010) *The Four Immeasurables: Practices to Open the Heart*. Boston: Shambhala Publications.

Walsh, C. (2010) 'Development as Buen Vivir: Institutional Arrangements and (de) Colonial Entanglements.' *Development*, 53(1): 15–21.

Waziyatawin and Yellow Bird, M. (2012) *For Indigenous Minds Only: A Decolonization Handbook*. Santa Fe: School for Advanced Research Press.

Weaver, D. (2008) 'Transforming Universities: The Expediency of Interculturality for Indigenous Superior Education in Ecuador.' Masters Thesis, Tulane University.

Weisbrot, M. (2015) 'Why Ecuador Loves Rafael Correa.' *The Guardian*, 15 February.

Wente, M. (2007) 'The Charitable and the Cheap: Which One Are You?' *Globe and Mail* online. 20 January.

Westheimer, J. (2010) 'Higher Education or Education for Hire? Corporatization and the Threat to Democratic Thinking.' *Academic Matters,* April–May. Ontario Confederation of University Faculty Associations.

Whitney, W. T. (2016) 'Clouds Gather over Bolivia's Change Process as US Intervenes.' *Counterpunch,* 16 February.

Yun, S. (2014) 'Accidental Death of a Poet.' *London Review of Books* online, 11 November.

Žižek, S. (2009) *First as Tragedy, Then as Farce.* London: Verso.

INDEX